WHY YOU SHOULD READ THIS LONG-ASS SHIT

SO ONCE UPON A TIME, I tried to convince a publisher to take this book. I had been waiting all my life to write a book like this.

All I needed now was Editor Scissorhands chopping out the clever parts.

Dorko the Designer looking for the Graffiti font on his computer.

And McClumsy in Marketing sending me on a reading tour of Hip-hop Malls...

"Who's your audience?" the publisher wanted to know. Already we were off to a bad start.

"I have in mind about ten different audiences for this book," I said. "First there's the oldschoolers who want to break away from what has become hip-hop. Then there's the hitchhikers who have the patience to organize a political movement, middle class white kids who want to move to the ghetto, ghetto kids who think rap is too stupid, graffiti writers who think graffiti is too boring, journalists who are disgusted with journalism, political activists who are sick of politics, freight-hoppers who give a damn about morality, business stiffs who don't give a damn about money or fashion, scholars who think books are dull, and street kids who think TV won't teach them anything they care to know. I belong to all of these audiences and I want *Bomb the Suburbs* to speak to all of them at once."

The publisher stared at me over the phone.

"KRS-ONE pulled it off on *By All Means Necessary*. People were coming out of nooks and crannies for that record. It brought together a new audience."

"Why don't you make a CD?" said the publisher.

He hung up the phone.

Consider it a miracle this book got to you. Me and my friends did it ourselves. The distribution and publicity need help so if you like the book, order ten more copies as birthday presents for everyone you know. Twenty if you live in the suburbs.

WILLIAM UPSKI WIMSATT
October 1994, Chicago

UNEK

Sixth Printing: 38,000 copies in print

Second Edition 2000
Layout by Stacy Wakefield
All art © copyright the artists
Printed in Canada

ISBN: 1887128-44-5

DECENTRALIZED WHOLESALE!

Soft Skull titles are available at 55% off for orders of ten books or more. Use our books as fundraising tools for good causes. We want to empower you to spread the word. Join the Soft Skull Decentralized Wholesale Program.

Send a check for the retail cost of 10 or more books (can be all one title, or a mix) minus 55%, plus $10 shipping, to the publisher at the following address:

Soft Skull Press, Inc.
98 Suffolk #3A
New York, NY 10002
www.softskull.com/wsale
sander@softskull.com

For book trade orders, please contact an exclusive distributor in your area:

USA AND CANADA:
> **Before January 1, 2001:**
> **Consortium Book Sales**
> tel. 800-283-3572

> **After January 1, 2001:**
> **Publisher's Group West**
> tel. 800-788-3123

AUSTRALIA:
> **Wakefield Press**
> tel. 61.8.8362.8800
> info@wakefieldpress.com.au

EUROPE:
> **Turnaround**
> tel. 44.020.8829.3000
> claire@turnaround-uk.com

CONTENTS

(Resist the temptation to read these out of order)

PAGE 2   **Introductions**

Subway scholar

Our most abused phrases

Rap music's identity crisis

Why do you want to bomb the suburbs?

They're saying tecs, we're saying technology:
   An interview with Reginald Jolley

PAGE 22   **Wiggers**

"We use words like 'Mackadocious'"
   [and other progress from the front lines of
   The White Struggle]

In defense of wiggers

Aren't you in the wrong neighborhood?

Hadn't I just been a special white boy?

PAGE 42   **Writers**

A job opening in Cleveland [I'm not even
gonna talk about the train yards]

Message to Mario: Wear your mask

Out over the stairwell

Dear Steven: Hip-hop is not a way of life—
   This is a warning!

If graffiti was rap

Dear Kozak: The rules of graffiti

PAGE 57   **Journalists**

Confessions of a super-groupie: An interview
   with Lesley Thomas

Letters to Victor—Yo Editor!—Dear Dry-Paper

PAGE 80   **Rappers**

Faking the conversation

The Chicago syndrome

How not to be taken advantage of:

An interview with Aaron Brown
The renegades of hip-hop—A music with little
  culture and no politics of its own
The coolest job in the world:
  An interview with Wendy Day

PAGE 102 **Chicago**

The urban frontier: a guided tour through one of
  Chicago's best kept secrets
Warp's legacy and my stupid one
Why Chicago is the only place that has
  all-city hip-hop meetings
Shane, 38, the great American homesteader
They don't take Mastercard and they don't take
  American Express
The truly illmatic: hip-hop and mental illness
The city that revived breakdancing

PAGE 126 **Roads & Rails**

"You can't hitchhike today": Kindness
  and generosity on the American road
They'll knife you in your sleep
Ride from a black woman
Stations on the national subway:
  A third wave of graffiti sweeps America

PAGE 142 **Conclusions**

Bomb the suburbs
Suckers don't last a minute:
  Good rhyme, bad theory
Hip-hop is supposed to eliminate itself: An
  interview with Super LP Raven
Minister Farrakhan, meet the Beastie Boys
  [okay, both of you can go now]
In search of hip-hop's moral center
Why this book is so dope

BOMB THE SUBURBS.

ANTCK

SUBWAY SCHOLAR

It was supposed to say "SUBWAY SCHOLAR." Riding the Jackson Park–Englewood El train on the South Side of Chicago, it was the last landmark you'd see before plunging into the subway downtown. Two-and-a-half stories up, spanning the backs of four factory buildings, in blockbuster letters too close and too big to ignore, you—no matter where you were—would read it: S-U-B-W-A- . . .

One night last week I was up there working on the "O". The "O" was on a building all by itself, an entire landing of the fire escape. Earlier that day, I had stood with janitor clothes, an orange reflector vest, a yellow hard hat and two gallons of white priming paint. I pretended I was painting over the graffiti. When the trains came by, I would wave to the motormen. A lot of them waved back.

So there I found myself that night, waiting for the bus, wearing white shorts and T-shirt, carrying bags across the city to a dark industrial alley with trains thundering overhead.

Some of my friends were supposed to come, especially Chris, but Chris backed out because there were supposed to be thunderstorms. I didn't mind painting in a thunderstorm. The better not to be noticed.

I climb the fire escape still wearing all-white. Cloudy sky, no sign of rain. I take my all-black painting clothes out of the bags, pull them on over the whites and strap a mask across my face. I feel warm and invisible in the night.

Which is a stupid way to feel. I've been caught painting up here before. The police check the alley with search lights, especially this fire escape which is the main way writers climb up onto the tracks. So every time a train comes by, which is every couple minutes until about 2 AM, sometimes around curves, sometimes up from the subway, the fire escape is lighted up and I have to run down and crouch out of view of the motorman.

So I'm up there painting the inside of the "O" for like half an hour. It's around midnight—I'm painting this scene of this girl playing in an overgrown lot—when I'm caught off guard by this worker train. The city's been doing track repairs all summer. A couple of times a night, worker trains stop up here, sometimes for twenty minutes, and do God-knows-what-I-never-stick-around-to-find-out.

I creep down the fire escape part way, curl up behind my paint bags and try to pass for a shadow should a cruiser decide to turn into the alley. I'm frozen there for a few minutes tryna be patient when I get the impulse to check behind me. Next to the fire escape, ten feet below me and ten feet to the rear, is this freight train embankment that I sometimes use as an escape route. And right there, right on the edge of the embankment is a scraggly-looking man crouching perfectly still, looking up at me, smoking a cigarette. So here we are in this abandoned alley in the middle of nowhere. I'm staring this guy down and he's staring me down. Ten seconds go by and neither of us moves. I can't see his face very well. There's a cigarette in front of it. Suddenly he stands up and with the flash of a pocket camera he tries to take a picture of me. I barely turn in time to hide my face.

So I'm like who the fuck is this guy? How long has he been here? What does he want? And what makes it weird, a similar thing happened the night before. I was lying in the same place and this bum enters the alley maybe 150 yards beyond the freight embankment. He leans against a supporting beam, stands there about fifteen minutes, smokes a cigarette looking right at me, and then he leaves—without seeing me. I had thought.

And what makes it weirder, a week before, we were painting the "SCH." It was me, Chris, and this fifteen-year-old kid I brought along named Finesse. It would have been bad enough if Finesse was his graffiti name. It was the name his parents gave him. When the trains would come, me and Chris would all be hiding in these crevices down the tracks. Finesse's ass wouldn't even hide. He would just keep playing on the fire escape, being all loud, borrowing cans to write his ugly, wack name everywhere, being all theatrical and shit. So finally, I get mad. I make him climb up the fire escape and wait for us on the roof. Then everything's cool for a minute. We're painting. Painting. Painting. All of a sudden, Finesse comes hurtling off the roof in a panic.

Oh Lord. Here he comes again.

"There's a body on the roof. A body on the roof. A dead body."

"Finesse," I say. "Leave. Me. The Fuck. Alone."

"NO. No NoNoNo. I'm serious. I'm serious. There's a body. I'm serious. I'm not joking. You gotta believe me. I ain't going up there."

We all climb up onto the roof. "There it is," Finesse says, pointing into a dark corner. Sure enough, there are the outlines of a body slouched in the darkness.

We tiptoe up to it. It doesn't move. We try talking to it. It doesn't move. We try kicking it. It still doesn't move. All of a sudden, here's Finesse. A beam of some kind is shooting out of Finesse and landing on the body. Finesse is pissing on the body!

"The fuck are you doing!" I yell.

Finesse is not pissing on the body. Finesse is spraying mace on the body. He got it out of my jacket which I let him wear.

Oh shit. The body moves. Oh shit. The body moves again. Oh shit. The body is coming back to life. Finesse has maced the body back to life. We push each other down the fire escape. We're on the tracks arguing, tryna figure out what to do. A police car spots us and tilts its search beam at us. We scatter into the night.

We never figured out who the body was. So here I am one week later. I scramble the cans into my bag, racking my brain about the scraggly guy. Is he a stealth cop? A vagabond trying to collect the reward for my arrest? Is he The Body? I'm throwing stuff in my bag and I'm watching him. He's very agile. He hops down from the freight embankment by this special way I thought only graffiti writers knew about. And then he does something else. He runs toward the base of the fire escape.

I grab my mask, dash up the fire escape, and vault onto the tracks. My escape route from here has been planned but the worker train is right there on the tracks (part of the set-up?). I've already been seen, but they're gonna have to catch me. I leap across the tracks, across the gaps and third rails, till I get to the catwalk, which lies in between the center tracks, and leads into the mouth of the subway two blocks away. All of this happens in seconds. I flee down the catwalk as fast as any man being chased. The catwalk is two feet wide, flanked on either side by a third rail. There is a rumbling behind me. Train. I jump over to the other track. I know the driver has seen me but he doesn't stop. I follow the red tail lights into the mouth of the tunnel, whipping off my gloves and tossing them, along with my mask, into crevices along the wall. The headquarters of the Chicago Police Department are exactly two blocks away.

Inside the subway tunnel, they have constructed a new subway line, not yet in service, which branches off from the tunnel I'm in and opens out into an even more abandoned district over by the river—a perfect getaway. I run the new tunnel, which is longer than I expect, and clean. There are no tags in it yet. I'm still looking over my shoulder for the scraggly guy, even though

ANTCK

there's no way he could have followed me—probably too many Freddy the 13th movies where the monster keeps jumping out at you just when you thought you were safe. I hop the razor wire, stash my black clothes (bad guys wear black), and follow the freight tracks across the river at 16th Street. I still haven't heard any police sirens. It's a big-cloud night and the whole Chicago skyline is lighted up like a dozen blocks away. I'm thinking now my whole mission is ruined and I won't be able to finish it before I go on the road. I'm thinking I gotta bring a posse up the next night and settle things with this dude.

Finally, I reach a busy street, Halsted. There's bus fare in my shoe. I take the Halsted bus to 55th, then the 55th Street bus home. All I can think is Whew.

No whew. There is a cop car on my corner. It sits there for five minutes. I retrieve my keys from a stash spot and when I return, the cop car is still there. I don't have any paint on my hands, I'm dressed like I go to Oberlin. There's no way they know I did anything. I walk past the cop car and I stare the cops down and they stare me down and I go into my apartment, shower, eat, congratulate myself on the escape and curse myself for losing the cans. Then I try to fall asleep. My parents are out of town.

At 3:15, I'm still awake. I keep thinking about that cop car on my corner, and about my friend who had to flee to California because the cops were doing intelligence on him trying to set him up. And I have this faint feeling that as I was running away from the scraggly guy, he was yelling my name. Biiilllyy. Biilllyyy.

And then I realize something that makes me sit up in bed. One of the bags I left on the fire escape had pockets in it which I didn't check. And suppose one of those pockets had something in it with my name on it. We are the only Wimsatt in the telephone book. And what if those cops on the corner were waiting there to testify that Yes I did come home at 2 am. And what if, at this very moment, they were preparing to bust in on me and search my house?

Spread out in my room are seventy spray cans. Many of them are rare brands—the same rare brands I left on the fire escape. Frantically, I run around hiding the paint in shopping bags behind clothes in my mother's closet, under dusty boxes in my father's study, and I'm running around the apartment with half the lights on, spray cans everywhere, when I hear someone clomping up the stairs. Clomp Clomp Clomp, I hear and I have pretty quiet neighbors, and I think for sure It's The Police. Why did I turn on the lights! The clomps come up to my door, then continue up the stairs. They're surrounding me, are they? A key turns in one of my upstairs neighbor's locks and I sigh a temporary relief. Unless . . . the neighbors are in on it too. I knew they were after me.

Two minutes later, the phone rings. 3:34 am. My plan is to sound like I'm half-asleep. ("The police at this hour? Whatever you want it can wait 'till the morning. Click.") I'm not sure how doing this will help, but I picture it playing an important role in some desperate future court case.

"Hello," I yawn falsely.

"Billy!" my friend Chris shouts into the phone. "It was me. It was me."

I croak in disbelief.

"It didn't rain, so I decided to come piece with you. I thought you recognized me. I started taking pictures of you but you ran away from me, I kept shouting 'Billy, it's Chris.' But you kept running, I thought you got killed by that train."

We never finished the piece.

(1992)

OUR MOST ABUSED PHRASES

BLUNT: an essential art form in the hip-pot culture. other art forms include twistin a cap off a 40, driving down the strip looking for a party, and shootin fake niggas wit a gat. (*See also* chronic; endo.)

FROM THE STREETS: except when used by the homeless. even then it's usually more like "on the sidewalk".

HOOD: especially when used to describe a neighborhood where one does not actually reside.

FAT, PHAT: suggested replacements: pork, lard, crisco, nabisco, REPRESENT.

FLAVOR: *see* mad.

MAD: mad flavor hoodies with the phat blunts beats beats be boomin in the jeeps jeeps . . . I'm from the STREETS.

OLD-SCHOOL: ah shut up you old wino, you isn't old-school. if you is, then why is you still so WACK?

FUCK NEW YORK: especially when every phrase, move, and style you use to dis New York City was invented

7

there.

FIVE-O: Please make up a new word. How're you going to yell "FIVE-0!" when they sit around like: "Hey 5-0, bring me a cup uh coffee and another custard-filled." "No Problem 5-0."

GAT: at least don't brag about it you little bitch.

SKINS: anything you wouldn't call your mother or your sister . . . "Yo c'mere honey dip, so I can wish you a Happy Mother's Day an shit. I bought you some of that moisturizing cream for dem skins, bitch."

GRAFFITI: unless it's illegal. Ain't no such thing as a graffiti T-shirt.

DOPE, DEF, FRESH, FLY, ALL THAT, ALL GOOD: Here At The Hip-hop Palace-Emporium we have a wide selection of street adjectives to choose from. You have so many choices.

PRACTICE WALL: waste o' paint. (*see also* hall of fame)

ANY WORD BEGINNING WITH "PH" OTHER THA "PHONE": any unjustifiable misspelling. Justifiable on include (1) Phelt Jam who uses the "ph" instead of "f" t get better letters to bomb with (2) "Phuck" as used b *Rappages* to bleep cusses (3) Bonz Malone, when he cre atively misspells so as to capture a voice—and because he it back in 1988 at *NYC* magazine (4) Phase 2 because it's part of his lifelong mission to undermine every aspect of western civilization.

SKILLS, CLEVER, ORIGINAL: especially when "able to keep a beat," "cheaply metaphorical," or "heard it before," would do just fine.

REAL/TRUE/TRUE TO THE GAME/FAKE/PHONY: if you even have to say it . . . ya know what I'm sayin?

YA KNOW WHAT I'M SAYIN?: no, what are you saying?

UNDERGROUND: except as used to describe (1) a writer who never airbrushes or does permissions (2) a b-boy who never appears in a video (3) an MC or DJ who never obtains a big show or a record deal (4) a wanted criminal

COMMERCIAL: spoken from the mouth of anyone who has a record deal.

REVOLUTIONARY: especially when "rebellious," "pissed-off," or "salty," would do.

HIP-HOP, HIP-HOPPER: except to mean someone who does or is two or more of the following: (1) bomb (2) b-boy or flex (3) MC (4) make beats—and can back that shit up in a battle.

THE HIP-HOP NATION: As Boots from The Coup writes: "What is all this 'hip-hop nation' shit I keep hearing about lately? 'Hip-hop nation' is a grouping of people based solely on the strategies of major record labels . . ."

HIP-HOP CORPORATION: especially when "corporation" by itself would do just fine.

RAP MUSIC'S IDENTITY CRISIS

Hip-hop is so confusing these days. I don't know what it is anymore, and I don't know whether I'm for it or against it.

Why only five years ago, hip-hop fans weren't just interested in skills and beats, we felt we were somehow part of—imagine this!—a righteous cause. Chuck D was going to train five thousand black leaders in five years. KRS-ONE was going to write a book and distribute zillions of free copies to every man, woman, and child. The words "master plan" showed up in every other rhyme and the words "sell out" actually carried some weight.

Nowadays, there's no such thing as a sell-out. Rappers have established that they are not role models and therefore they don't owe anything to anyone.

Hip-hop used to move me. It doesn't move me anymore. Gone are the days when hip-hop was a matter of honor, something to show and prove, something to change your life around for. Now hip-hop has to change itself for you. It has no politics and little culture of its own. It means all things to all people—its most precise anthem is "Doowutchulike"—anything goes, anything is acceptable.

Something we hold as dear as hip-hop cannot exist in the eyes of

the beholder alone. Hip-hop itself must mean something. If we cannot say what hip-hop means then who are we as hip-hoppers? Rap music's identity crisis is a reflection of our individual identity crises. To ask what rap stands for is to ask ourselves what we stand for.

And if rap stands for nothing then it has no protection against the forces which are infiltrating it and making it theirs. As a mere reflection of the larger society, it falls easy prey to society's problems. The failure of rap to define itself according to its own standards is the central crisis of rap today.

Over the coming century, hip-hop will be resurrected (Thank you Common Sense) and rejuvenated many more times before it ever seriously begins to stagnate.

But looking back on the mid-'90s, after we have rubbed the star dust out of our eyes and coughed the blunt clouds from our throats, the really important things in life will remain: love, raising children, economic security, emotional insecurity, a worthwhile job, being a decent person, etc. All of that will still be there. It just won't be in most of the music.

For those who want to bring back a greater purpose to hip-hop music and culture, don't be discouraged. Your time will return within the next couple of years. People can't go forever without some higher purpose in their lives. Now is when to lay the foundation.

WHY DO YOU WANT TO BOMB THE SUBURBS?

I say bomb the suburbs because the suburbs have been bombing us for at least the last forty years. They have waged an economic, political, and cultural war on life in the city. The city has responded by declaring war on itself.

Bomb the Suburbs is a message to people who live in the city. It is a call to change your strategy. Stop bombing the city. Stop bombing the ghetto. Stop fucking up your own neighborhoods and taking your frustrations out on those around you.

People who live around you are not the root cause of your problems. The people who are most responsible for your problems don't live anywhere around you and they don't intend to live anywhere around you.

Bomb the Suburbs means let's celebrate the city. Let's celebrate the ghetto and the few people who aren't running away from it. Let's stop fucking up the city. Let's stop fucking up the ghetto. Let's start defending it and making it work for us.

If we have frustrations, we should direct them to people who don't have any real frustrations of their own, people who are so fucking spoiled and so fucking isolated, they don't even realize how spoiled and isolated they are.

Of course we're going to get angry at our families, our friends, that set over there, the teacher, the police officer. But let us remember these problems wouldn't be nearly as bad if it weren't for the everyday cowardice which causes certain people to avoid the whole area where we live, hoarding their resources to themselves.

For all the pain they've caused us, the suburbs deserve to be bombed literally. We're not going to do that. We just want you fuckers out there to understand a few things.

1. You have problems. One of your problems is that you don't know how to deal with us.

2. You need to stop running away from your problems. It makes them worse for us.

3. We're going to start making it worse for you. We're going to keep confronting you. If you run away from us, we're going to keep coming after you.

4. You may be able to avoid us temporarily, but you will not be able to avoid the thought of us. The price of avoiding us is the fullness of your humanity. And we'll still haunt you with music, our graffiti, and anything else we thow at you when backed into a corner. Your children will cuss you out in language they learn from us.

Gentle readers, please note, the title is "Bomb the Suburbs", not "Bomb the Suburbanites." We don't hate *you*. We do hate the way you behave, especially when it ends up hurting people like us and our friends.

You have been trying to tell us to change for a long time. You lecture us about the social pathology of the inner city and how we need to become more like you. We need to move to the suburbs too. We

need to pull ourselves up by the bootstraps and abandon our "undesirables" the way you abandoned us.

We need to do this. We need to do that.

We're not the ones who did the most to create the problems. We're trying to face the problems you left us with. We're staying behind and trying to make things better.

We think the suburbs are what needs to be changed about America. We think the suburbs are bad for America.

Socially, they intensify segregation and mistrust. Culturally, they erode the sense of history, narrow the outlook, and dull the imagination. Economically, they intensify inequality by isolating the rich and poor. Then the poor lack access to good schools, hospitals, businesses, police, transportation, city services, concerned neighbors, and any of the things that would allow them to alleviate their situation. The rich lack access to reality and any sense of proportion. They run around in a comfort warp, taking everything for granted and misusing what they have.

The century of the city was 1880-1980. The coming century will be the century of the suburb. We haven't even begun to imagine the new suburbs-based America. City and country alike will be overrun with parking lot architecture. Sidewalks, buses, trains, and other relics of public space will continue to disappear. The distinctiveness, character, and history of the landscape will be washed corporately clean. Security guards and alarm systems will protect almost everything (except for the lives of the poor). Downtowns will become malls.

The ghetto will continue spreading into the suburbs. Ghettos of the next century will look less like the South Side and more like East St. Louis: bankrupt little shanty-towns. Isolated, without bus routes, libraries, or trash collection.

Suburbanization is not only one of the most important trends of the coming century. It is one of the most important metaphors for where our heads are at these days. Everybody wants to go off with their own group, do their own thing, cut themselves off from everyone else, and cease to be accountable. Every possible sub-group now has its own inward-looking magazine and organization.

I want to live in an America without ghettos or suburbs.

THEY'RE SAYING TECS, WE'RE SAYING TECHNOLOGY

Reginald Jolley started breakdancing in 1983. He never stopped.

REGINALD: I'm staying in tune with what used to be hip-hop. If LA is gonna do commercial rap and New York is gonna follow, then my job is to stay in tune with what it was. You know . . . lyrics—how it used to be. Actually written down, clever lyrics and beats. Beats that work. You're not working if you sample More Bounce to the Ounce. Please. What else can you do?

It used to be that you could quote the lyrics of rap music, like Rakim. Nowadays, people think Snoop or Dre or the rest of Compton are writing clever lyrics. He said he'll take your mama out—that's dope! It's funny how being wack is dope now. Trendy things and biting and gimmicks is dope. You got all these clowns. Videos messed rap up. Before you had to judge the lyrics. What he was saying. Now you're selling a picture. It's all about the image. And now it's to a point where rap won't be rap no more. It will all just be gangster stuff, and marijuana hippie stuff—that will be rap.

These people are clowns. Ice-T, Spice 1, MC Eight, Breed, Tupac. What they try to say is yeah, y'all into that soft rap. Please! Gangsta rap is commercial rap. The first formula for commercial rap was smiling and acting innocent—Young MC, Hammer, etc. Now the formula is taking the happy beats—Dre's production which is not hip-hop at all—and to put it with the savage lyrics.

So what are you doing?
Adding to my money clip, cleaning my jewelry and buying sneakers. The company I keep, The Dariens, we're screaming '88. I just use that time bracket because it was memorable. That was when hip-hop was talking about having fun. A group was on MTV talking about bringing back '88. How you gonna bring back '88 talking about blunts this, tecs that, tecs, tecs, tecs. '88 was about knowledge of self, doing for self, making it, being successful. That's why everyone's going back to rapping over Special Ed, Biz Markie, all the '88 hits. It wasn't no mainstream thing either. That was the real. The '93 vibe is corny. Like when did biting become cool? Onyx came out biting Busta Rhymes. It's cool. Funkdoobiest bit Das EFX. It's cool. Everybody bit Busta Rhymes. It's just accepted.

What other problems do you see?
Right now it's wack for guys and girls to dance at a party. You've got to frown. You can't have fun. That's the hip-hop face. A frown. Most people say that what I'm talking about is selling out . . . It's wack . . . Or any of those hip-hop words they say. Graffiti, just because it's illegal doesn't make it art. People try to say what I'm talking about is selling out because I said if you have any art talents go to school. In '88, rappers had songs about going to school. Biz, Diamond Shell. Large Professor. Watch Roger do his thing—that was Darien-like.

Once gangsta rap came out, it made all the gangbangers like rap. They used to dis us. They used to call it breakdancing music. Gangsta rap crossed the thugs into it. Now, for instance, you got the guy that's watching MTV with an afro and a pick in his hair and boots questioning me like you better get up on hip-hop. I'm like, "Clown, I made you." People like me don't count no more. That's how you get Dre rated album of the year. That shit is wack. It's because of the masses who never were into rap until gangsta rap came out. The Gargoyle crowd even changed because of gangsta rap. They felt like pussies doing vocabulary rhymes. Clever rhymes.

You know what's funny though. There are people in control who know it's wack but doin' it anyway. *The Source*, WHPK. Shit that didn't have shit to do with hip-hop . . . Ant Banks . . . Bass . . . Carry that shit on. For *The Source* to know it's wack! Rappers that were once doing hip-hop, MC Lyte, Kool G. Rap, Big Daddy Kane, PRT, Brand Nubian, now they're doing Hollywood. Now Cool J and RUN-DMC are talking about shooting people. I guess Chuck D will be talking about it next. People like me are giving in. It's political now. When an artist is hot, you can't say they're wack 'cause it'll mess you up. You'll have to say they're dope when you do an interview. And then just change the subject.

You've been ahead of your time on a lot of things. What do you think is gonna happen from here?
What I think is gonna happen now. Pretty soon gangster is not gonna be enough. It's gonna be Let's do straight-up evil. Like Headbanger by EPMD, Red Man with that 666. Rappers wearing hard rock T-shirts. Rap is gonna be black heavy metal. Horror rap.

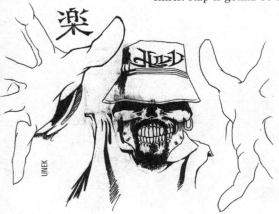

Yeah, like JP Chill was saying, in 1987, Chuck D said rap was the CNN *of black youth. Today rap has become the* Hard Copy/Current Affair/Cops *of black youth.*
The era where I'm from, hip-hop names were like Slick Rick, Biz Markie. Fresh this. Def that. MC this. MC that. Now hip-hop names are Old Dirty Bastard, Ghostface Killer, Flatliners. Look at Cypress Hill's logo. Skulls and hatchets and blood for the type—which are used in many rapper's logos.

Rumplestilskinz. My attitude is fucked-up and real shitty.
Please. A lot of people on wax don't even know as much about hip-hop as people in Chicago. The camp that I'm with has always said Treach was wack. Now that he dissed Tung Twista, everybody's saying that he's wack. We always said he was wack. We're into lyrics and beats. We're business-minded. We've always pushed what's true. We're not rushing people with demos.
    When Schooly D and Just Ice and KRS-ONE were doing gangsta rap, it wasn't like let's act this out in life. People are getting too wrapped up in the character they portray. They go into the studio and become this fictional character that doesn't go to jail. Spice 1. None of these people write. Throw on an instrumental. Now rap. Special

16

Ed, Biz Markie, Pete Rock and CL Smooth, Tribe Called Quest, Grand Puba, Diamond D, Gang Starr. They all do hip-hop. Kool G Rap writes. I think Akinyele writes. He says: I'm not a director so don't come over here acting up. He says: My name is heroin. Keep my name in vein. That's writing.

What about Chicago?
Chicago, we've been here. Of course we don't get the credit because we have the reputation of being a follower city. Right now, I see Chicago rap going with this whole ill-mannered gangster stuff. Chicago needs to broaden its horizons. Let's pretend to have a Zulu Nation. Let's pretend to have *The Source*. You can't make a mark like that. Drink the 40s and blunts and stuff later. You can't be blunted, talking about hip-hop while we looking over some lawyer's papers. Make your money first, then celebrate. Rap is so savage now. The camp I'm with, we represent the real hardcore. What hardcore used to mean. Divine Force, Dismasters, Ultramag, JVC Force, Masters of Ceremony, old Mantronix.

People think representing Chicago means saying Fuck LA. Fuck New York. What do you mean? That's not how you rap by saying fuck other cities. I don't like LA rap, and I don't like a lot of New York rap, but I'm not going to make songs about it on demos or records. You don't ask for props. You just do dope shit. All that energy wasted on Y'all and New York. Later for that.

Tell me about breakin.
Breakdancing was, you know, real dope. I loved the old-school and I'm glad we held onto it. New York thought it was old and wanted to move on. We kept doing it. During the Alcatraz, I felt so good 'cause it was underground again. I got my own thing that nobody knows about. Back in the day, we would go to house parties and battle house dancers. Once it went commercial, now that it's so-called back, I leave it alone now. Crazy Legs is in every issue of *The Source*. Once it dies back down, I'll be into it again.

Neatness has always been important. Sloppiness has always been wack. People dance like a maniac slave that's been let out of a cage. A barn. Goin crazy kicking girls in the chest. My moves go in order. That's why it looks crisp.

What people don't know is that old-school look was really through LA because of techno. Punk Rock Techno grabbed hold of the old-school look because it was another rebellion for suburban kids. A lot of white fashions grasp older fashions. Just like the '60s look. The '70s look. Early '80s. They're saying: I'm a b-boy character. I'm something I'm not. There ain't no such things as hip-hop clothes. It never has been. After Troop came out and we realized we played ourselves. Please. Pass me a Fendi watch, a Gucci link. This is real b-boy shit. Talk to me about Scott La Rock pulling up in an all-black BMW.

People are always talking about unity. What do you make of that?
When you say unity what do you mean? The foundation of it is support. Chicago feels that we don't support Chicago. We support what we think is hip-hop. I remember going up to WHPK seeing these people who were writing lyrics. Then they come sampling gunshots. I'm like, Damn, don't I remember you from the Gargoyle? Didn't you used to write lyrics? I'm from an era when it was cool to look in the dictionary, to rap big words, to rap science. We let it get out of our hands and it's our fault.

A real b-boy won't buy Onyx or Funkdoobiest . . . or Cash Money Marvelous. When it was bit, it wasn't supported. A perfect example is Arrested Development. They bit the hell out of the Jungle Brothers. When it's bit, you just don't buy it.

B-boys were inner city kids who were trying to get theirs. Cazals were glasses, ugly as hell. Same with shell toes. But they had gold on the side. You wanted things you weren't supposed to have. Like *Wild Style*. Busy Bee rapping in the back seat of a limo. That's hip-hop. All this ghetto this and I ain't never gonna make it. I grew up hard. AHHRR. I chew off your mama's arm. Please. The Darien way is about making the money we never had—and doing it legally.

Why legally?
I had family into that drug thing. It's a foolish way. It ain't real.

Okay, personal question. You're considered smart. Even people who don't like you can see that much. At 24, you're probably the youngest Art Director at Burrell Advertising, which is the top black-owned ad firm in the country. Why did you go to Schurz High School? Why didn't you go to one of the magnet schools? Von Steuben or Lane or Whitney Young or somewhere?
I was trying to get into Lane and Whitney Young. My scores weren't

high enough.

Tell me about the Dariens. A lot of people dis you guys, wearing Polo, saying you're tryna be from New York or something.

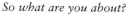

I know you've heard people say we're tryna act white. That's so funny to me. Please. You sleeping till 2 o'-clock talking about black this, black that. You a sell-out 'cause we live in the real world. As for the clothes, that doesn't even concern me. Dariens stay dipped. Never looking broke like the Liberty Bell cause that ain't swell.

So what are you about?
The Dariens, we're about having a direction. Being productive. Having a goal. Being on something the average black youth is not on. We don't drink 40s. We don't smoke blunts . . .

> They're saying tecs. We're saying technology.
> They're saying I'm psycho. We're saying psychology.
> They're saying what up G. We're saying geology.
> They're talking about Beat Street. We're talking about Wall Street.

What about these attempts to organize Chicago hip-hop? Chi-Rock? Zulu . . . Cashus D, you know . . .
I don't know about Chi-Rock. These new kids in Chi-Rock, they used to get dissed by Chi-Rock with the Dariens at the Darien parties. We were the backpack wearin, baggy pants wearin new jacks. The same kids are now yelling chapters at me while I'm on my lunch break. Please. I'm not in a hip-hop gang. I respect Cashus D. I respect him a lot.
Why not join Zulu?
I wanted to be in the Zulu Nation back in the day. There are so many negative rappers in it now. If Ice-T is in the Zulu Nation, it represents the opposite of what it represents to me. Ice-T? Huh? No need for me.

ANTCK

What would a hip-hop-based movement look like to you? Organizationally? Racially? What would it consist of? What would it be based on?

When it comes to race, hip-hop is at its core a black and Hispanic thing—when it comes to making up rules for it. When it gets social and political, when it's time to voice opinions and rebel, it's time to help the black man. When you go to hip-hop as a movement, it's gonna go to Black awareness. From Bambaataa to Clarence 13X to Malcolm X to The Honorable Elijah Muhammad, and so on. Hip-hop is a joke compared to that. Hip-hop isn't the real movement. They're all entertainers. And we don't control the entertainment industry so all artists can do is hold up picket signs and say the white man is the devil. Which is backwards. The industry says: What you're saying don't mean nothing to me because I got you. Hey, sell my record pal.

We tryna tell kids younger than us to go to school and stay focused. They're spending their time tagging and getting blunted in a so-called cipher while their white friends parents are saying, Benny is going through a phase. We'll put his college money to the side. This is real. That's why people don't like what we represent. We talking about working on the Macintosh, not wearing a Krylon cap around our neck. We're telling kids in high school that getting good grades is what's swell. The average crew is gonna tell them cutting class is dope. We take time to talk to them on the phone, or on the street, exercise the power of positive conversation. But we're not stronger than the TV.

Right now, America's teaching that we're just entertainment. Put the ball in. Carry the ball. Run with it. Make me laugh. Make me cry. Make me dance. But never in a situation where we're making decisions. A man bringing something to the table rather than the entertainment at lunch break.

Everyone is ready to react when it's in their face like if a black leader gets assassinated. That's the only time they can rebel. They can't prevent it. They can't trace the problem back. They don't have knowledge of self. They're afraid to succeed, to say I can do anything I want. The attitude should be: I'm gonna read up on it and do it.

What books? What books did you read?

Message to the Black Man. The Theology of Time. The Meaning of the

FOI. Eat to Live. This is what the Nation of Islam teaches. A lot of people take it as some old hate stuff. To me, that's not what it's saying. And that white man this and white man that is played out.

What got you into reading?
My uncle just gave me books and talked to me. I had a mom who acted like a mom. Then once you read some you get more curious and you just start studying on your own. What the Nation of Islam teaches is common sense. It teaches any human how to be a human. Especially blacks. To carry yourself with dignity. Screaming the white man is the devil is old. "Message to the Black man" was the name of the book. It wasn't called "Message to the White man." We need to be learning to be civilized, learning knowledge of self. Learning self-discipline so we can carry on like the rest of America.

The Dariens are talking about golf and mansions. I want to get a boat. Seriously man. I want to learn more about the world. See things I only read about. Who says I can't do this 'cause I'm black. Now, the law, even if they don't like me, they would have to assist me because of their own law. You just have to work hard. Working hard is the norm. Going the extra mile is the norm.

So what's gonna happen now with hip-hop?
People are realizing rap is messed up. '93 was a wack year. The whole year was wack. *The Source* was talking about the hype over Snoop Doggy Dog. Now they're saying Nas' shit is dope—which it is. But they helped hype Snoop. Don't point the finger. I'm hoping this gangster shit just gets played out 'cause people are starting to get tired of it. Rap is going against what the Zulu Nation stands for. What brought Zulu into existence was to put a stop to the gangs and have peace to do art. Hip-hop has become totally the opposite of what created it. Zulu was about Peace, Unity, Love, and Having Fun. What's going on now is about Violence, Disorganization, Self-hate, and . . . Glorifying bad times.

Fuck that. The Dariens are on mode baby. Pass the ginger ale, the money sack, and the Real Estate section 'cause I got the jewels.

"WE USE WORDS
LIKE MACKADOCIOUS"

One Saturday last summer, Josh and Eric, college students from Birchhead, Georgia put on some Cross Colours and old school Adidas to wear to a neighborhood which Josh described as "kind of scary . . . almost like a ghetto." The neighborhood was downtown Atlanta. Jaws stiffened, hats backward, they hit the city hoping—for what they weren't quite sure—to fit in, to earn respect, to participate in a lifestyle they had admired for years on TV. Unsure what to do with themselves, they shopped and ate lunch. They didn't talk to anyone; they barely even talked to each other. "It felt like the black people were laughing at us," they said later.

Sabrina Williams, 20, of Miami Beach, Florida. would have liked to talk to them. "When I see whites doing that, I quiz them," says Sabrina, also a college student when she's not working or trying to keep her mom off crack. "When they don those clothes, to me it's like they're donning a costume, just like if they was to smear black paint on they face. They're degrading my culture. They're saying anyone can do this.

"They don't understand the swagger, the way we walk, the way we talk. It comes from when you don't have self-esteem, okay, you try to mask it. You say, 'Hey I might not be smart but I'm cool.' All you've got is your coolness. Being cool isn't something you do. It's

GTEK

something you feel. Here come all these little white people who never had to live with that shit."

Like it or not, whites seem to be buying rap in increasing numbers. Nameless Noodlebrains of The Industry estimate that when a rap record goes gold, whites constitute at least half of the sales.

This has advanced rap's clout, capital, and potential to transform society. But the white audience doesn't just consume rap, it shapes rap also. Rappers and record labels aren't stupid. They know who's listening and the music gets tailored to the audience.

Increasingly, rappers address their white audience, either directly, by accommodating our perceived tastes, targeting us for education/insult, or indirectly, by shunning the white audience, retreating into blacker, realer, more hardcore stances—all the more titillating for their inaccessibility.

With rappers defining themselves in relation to the white audience, the biggest topic in rap right now seems to be rap itself. To understand where hip-hop is going, then, we must understand this white audience. Hitchhiking America this summer, I met dozens of these young peckerwoods and here's what I found.

The white rap audience is as diverse as the music itself: from the trench-coat hood outside a liquor store in Montgomery who I almost fought because he "dint trust no white repotuh"—to Michael, an effeminate wimp who shrieks "Sang it Sistaaa Soujahhh!" as he traces the cul-de-sacs of suburban St. Louis in his parent's car with the windows rolled up "so we don't get bothered by ignorant people".

Then you have special interest groups. Metal-heads dig the hard beats. Parents like the R&B, up-tempo stuff. Ideologues buy the rappers who confirm their political world view. Teens get off on the coolness and the sex. Intellectuals appreciate the poetry. Musicians go for Gang Starr—and likewise for every conceivable taste. When they say they like rap, they usually have in mind a *certain* kind of rap, one that spits back what they already believe, or lends an escape from their little lives. The Hammer–Kris Kross audience is so filtered, they hardly identify themselves with rap at all.

Most are more normal. They discovered rap within the last four years. They like the bass. They like the attitude. They hate Vanilla Ice. They think it's unfair that they are *called* Vanilla Ice. They want to experience blackness, dramatic and direct (more so than fans of jazz or reggae)—but not too direct, thank you very much. Associating themselves with rap sends the desired message, whether it's "I want

23

some black dick," "I'm not racist," or simply "I'm cooler than the rest of you white motherfuckers!"

His first year at college, Martay the Hip-hop Wiz, an extremely nice and otherwise thoughtful Atlanta rapper who always had black friends in high school, sat at the black table in the cafeteria every day for three months. "I would sit there writing rhymes and listening to tapes, hoping to make some friends. I would even put the tapes on the table for them to see what I was listening to. But no one ever talked to me."

They were supposed to talk to him.

Sporting their rap gear and attitude serves to disguise white kids' often bland, underdeveloped personalities. Unlike the rappers they admire, many are shy and inarticulate.

"It seems to me that people with these characteristics would naturally be drawn to music that is made especially braggadoccious *just for them*," notes critic Tom Frank, who points to parallel behavior in punk rock fans who buy rebellious images in the form of consumer goods. "That's why so many ads talk about 'breaking the rules'."

If you ask them a question, they act like they're being tested. If someone accuses them of "acting black," they have a speech prepared. They mete out calculated, color-blind answers, and brag on how much struggle they've gone through—however little that is.

Even in Sheridan, Wyoming, the white rap kids ("wiggers") wear their X shirts and blast "Mistadobalina" or "Soul by the Pound" on the way to the strip mall, oblivious to the meaning, oblivious to the irony.

If you think nobody's that dumb, meet Brian and Laramie, 16-year-old, orange and green outfit matching, blond boys from Louisville, shoppers in the rap section of a record store.

"Rap is the style in our school," they take turns explaining (I swear I didn't make this up).

"When I pump it, it makes me feel like everybody can hear me. At school, it makes you more popular."

"I like the way the voice sounds. It gets you pumped up, gets you in a good mood."

"It's our favorite kind of music . . . We buy the clothes we see in videos . . . We use words like 'mackadocious'." Laramie grins.

"We have a lot of pro-black clothes," Brian adds more seriously.

Their favorite groups are Public Enemy, X-Clan, and Cypress Hill. "We like those groups because they have meaning. They're pro-black. They're fighting back against racism."

Do you ever think the rappers might be talking about you?

"It doesn't bother me, because it's not us who they're talking about. We think they're talking about someone else, about bigots, white politicians."

Brian and Laramie attend a fifty-fifty public school, but haven't been to a rap concert because "at concerts they beat up white people."

How do you know that?

"We just know . . . We've heard."

What if rap fades out and something else comes in?

"We'll probably stop listening to it," they reply in unison.

And because rap has gone mainstream, fans who consider themselves hardcore (everyone this side of Heavy D) have to prove to everyone, including themselves, just how down they are with hip-hop. They dis the Beastie Boys, then Shan, LL, Kane, all the way up to Public Enemy ("They fell off after the second album . . . got too established") and Das EFX ("Fuck that happy shit").

At the extreme they act like they helped invent the shit. "That's *our* music they tryna do out in California," says a wiggette who claims she's from Queensbridge. Yet even lifetime rap fans (excluding those who are ideological bitches for every supposed black cause) usually discount a crucial reason rap was invented: white America's economic and psychological terrorism against black people— reduced in the white mind to "prejudice" and "stereotyping," concepts more within our cultural experience.

Chris, 21, of Denver lives in a pick-up truck and has been dancing to hip-hop "since Mantronix first came out." Peep his wisdom: "I think everyone should just be equal, but the blacks are trying to be better than everyone else. They don't have it bad in this country. They just say gimme gimme gimme."

Chris isn't unusual. Many white rap fans feel this way.

Part of it is age. Frank, 23, of Queens likes rap, but he's not into it like his 19-and-20-year-old friends. "My generation grew up with Zeppelin, the next generation got into it through breakdancing."

Rap's greatest impact is on the youngest listeners. "I like the ghetto music. It's real tough in East LA," says Andrew, 11, a wide-eyed blond boy from posh North Naples, Florida where it is illegal to bounce basketballs because of the noise. "It shows white people's lives aren't as tough as theirs. Almost every song someone gets killed. Like the Geto Boys. He started out in a poor neighborhood." Andrew says that the older kids in his school don't like rap but the fifth, sixth, and seventh graders don't listen to anything else.

Sabrina's advice: "If you want to listen to rap, cool, but investigate it. Go to a ghetto. We're very open people, not like whites."

"I want them to be offended by rap music," says Sabrina. "Because I'm offended by them." But instead of taking offense at anti-white lyrics, many try to distance themselves from the target. In other words, they strive to be *down*.

Detroit suburbanite Jamie, 19, is a clerk at a record store. "I can relate to city life," he says. "Some of my friends were into drugs and fights. I mean . . ." he started to say, but his sentence trailed off. A black customer had entered the store. "W'sup man." Jamie greets him. For Alex, 18, the paradox goes further. After hoisting some Nikes and a machete during the LA Riots, he hailed a taxicab back home to Pasadena.

Hopefully more and more white kids are gonna start imitating gangsters. Then it'll get played out and black and Hispanic kids will stop shooting each other. ("Get that gun away from me you sell-out house nigga! Go talk to a white girl.")

When Holly Poopster* from the Chicago suburb of Evanston attended her first hip-hop party a year ago, she and her friend told me that they didn't feel accepted at the party because they were white. "We come from a very, very integrated community," she told me (Evanston is seventy-one percent white), as if to say, "It's not our fault they don't like us".

It has been a big year for Polly Schmooster! But don't call her Golly anymore. Her name is "Sista PA," and though she can't quite dance yet, she has befriended a bunch of dredlock b-boys, and feels welcome at parties. She writes passionately about breakdancing and stopping violence for *Dry-Paper*, a Chicago rap publication.

The Sista even uses words like "phunkyphatphresh" and plays blacker-than-thou with another white writer, me, saying I'm not hardcore. (Thought I'd return the favor, Hopsy. Next time you play that shit we're gonna battle.) Topsy has learned what all of us know, that most blacks will accept anyone who makes the slightest effort not to be a typical white asshole—or maybe Popsy's still back in the "I must be

---

* Whatever her name is. Somethin like that.

special" stage.

Wanting to be down but not wanting to sacrifice for it—the way blacks have to sacrifice to be down with us—that's the age-old story of whites in black culture (let alone every other culture on the planet). We fall in love with black culture and the deeper we get, the more we begin to hear with black ears, move with black limbs, see with black eyes. Over time and (what we imagine is much) tribulation, our striving grows less transparent, less offensive, harder to laugh at. Then we get jobs as documenters, marketers, and even creators of something that used to be black music.

One day the rap audience may be as white as tables in a jazz club, and rap will become just another platform for every white ethnic group—not only the Irish—to express their suddenly funky selves. In the meantime, every Josh, Eric, Martay, Brian, Laramie, Chris, Frank, Andrew, Jamie, Alex, Sista PA, and Upski of the white race plunges deeper into a debt that we have no intention of trying to repay.

This article was published in The Source (May '93). Published, that is, except for the last paragraph. It went like this:

Of course there are many ways to view whites' role in hip-hop, not all of them bad, and yes, we are individuals. But let me offer this advice to black artists: Next time y'all invent something, you had better find a way to control it financially, because we're going to want that shit. And since it's the '90s, you won't even get to hear us say "Thanks niggers."

"It's too mean-spirited," said my editor. "It's overkill . . . disrespectful . . . offensive . . . going to alienate people . . . unnecessary."
I thought about this for a minute.
"So is rap!" I said.
Half an hour of arguing won my paragraph a second chance around the office. Everybody still had a problem with it. My paragraph and I despaired. It was the key to the whole article, the only part that might give a few of us white boys our one precious glimmer of self-doubt. (I'm not too worried about what black people think. They've heard it all before.) Other white writers have tried to show white people how bad they are, but it doesn't work because the writer himself stays above the fray. Then all the reader has to do is identify with the writer and he's home-free, exempt from white supremacy. I let the reader know that I too am white supremacy.

IN DEFENSE OF WIGGERS

The Oprah people were on the phone with my mom. Someone had given them my name as an expert on wiggers. You know, wiggers. White kids scorned by their peers for listening to rap. I was an expert on that.

My mother and I were glad to hear that I was an expert on something. Even without the last paragraph, "We Use Words like Mackadocious" had become the most responded to article in the history of hip-hop journalism. The Oprah guy was on the phone, trying to size me up.

Oh, I'm not trying to ridicule wiggers, I told him. Merely to describe them would accomplish this. I have little interest in ridicule for its own sake. The very things I hate the most about The Wigger: his stupid audacity and perverted desire (deeply held and deeply denied) to be down with black people—these personality defects are a cause for celebration. If channeled in the right way, the wigger can go a long way toward repairing the sickness of race in America.

The Oprah guy thought about this for a moment. "We're trying to pick white hip-hop fans for the panel," he said. "How do you dress?"

How do I dress?

"Yeah, you know . . . Are your pants eight sizes too big . . ."

I didn't make the panel.

Remember the scene in Spike Lee's Malcolm X, where Malcolm-soon-to-be-X's Muslim mentor asks if he has ever known a good white person (Malcolm thinks about it and says he hasn't). Even a lot of whites who admire Malcolm X banished from their mind the implicit question: Would his answer have been any different had he known *me*?

Look, none of us is born knowing the best way to live in a place as racially loaded as America—let alone in the sub-society of hip-hop. I'm no great authority myself. But I have been around the block enough to pretty much know where the potholes are—if only because I've fallen in them so many times.

My own thoughts about race started pretty naively. Not that any-one would have thought to ask, but for moments in my early life I must have been under the impression that black people ruled the Earth. I owed this inverted world view to two contradictory sources.

One of these was the fashionable University of Chicago Labora-tory School where I was sent starting at age 2. Although more than 60% white, and located in the whitest section of the Hyde Park neigh-borhood, "Lab School" and its immediate community are a demo-graphic blip in the middle of Chicago's South Side, the largest and most populous black settlement in North America.

Minutes away are Pill Hill, The Gap, Prairie Shores, Chatham, Kenwood, Beverly, South Shore, and other enclaves of black prosper-ity where the likes of Muhammad Ali, Louis Farrakhan, Gwendolyn Brooks, Jesse Jackson, Carol Moseley Braun, R. Kelly, and Rashied Lynn (AKA Common Sense) have made their homes.

The Johnson Publishing family, the Burrell Advertising family, and U of C sociologist William Julius Wilson all sent their kids to Lab School. The 1993 keynote speaker for Black History Month was Bet-ty Shabazz (Malcolm X's widow), a close personal friend of one of the parents. Are you getting the picture? Many of the first blacks I en-countered were richer than I was. One of the boys seemed to come to school wearing an expensive new pair of shoes every other week—in the third grade!

Fifty-fifty Hyde Park, where I grew up two blocks from the apartment of Harold Washington, Chicago's first black mayor, was not all rich though. And it was surrounded by Woodlawn, Grand Boulevard, Washington Park and North Kenwood. These were some of the most messed-up neighborhoods in the city—places so rocked that many residents didn't know their neighborhoods had names. These were the birthplaces of Chicago's rival black street gangs, the ones that set the pattern of gang affiliations from Kansas City to Birm-

ingham to Cleveland for years before the infiltration of Bloods and Crips. These were the stomping grounds of Richard Wright's Bigger Thomas. The white family Bigger worked for, whose daughter he later killed, they lived—all of that was to have taken place—in my neighborhood. Before I understood the abstract powers of money, politics, and prestige, I understood the power of I-could-get-my-ass-kicked.

In the family car, we would sometimes have to drive through the ghetto—or past it if possible. God forbid our car should get stuck. From the back seat, I would peer out on the forbidding world beyond the boundaries of 47th Street, 61st Street, and Cottage Grove, fantasizing about what anarchy presided there amid the wrecked and neglected buildings.

James T. Farrell's short story "The Fastest Runner on 61st Street," written back when 61st was white, tells of a white boy gang from 61st Street spotting a black boy who had strayed across Washington Park. A chase ensues, and when the fastest of the gang crosses 51st Street into the black neighborhood he is killed instantly—within a block. In the logic of white Hyde Park, this was the only plausible result.

And in the summertime especially, the ghetto would drive, walk, bus, and bike through Hyde Park (if they were riding double, it meant they were planning to steal yours), in search of the museum, the beach, the theater, and the affluent aura. I still remember the first time I saw a white person walking in the ghetto. "Look, look , I saw a white lady." I shouted from the back seat. "She's probably a prostitute," my mom responded.

My early experience with race was more immediate than that of most whites, but the patterns were about the same. Blacks most likely to enter our world tend to be the socioeconomic extremes rather than the vast middle. Between the assimilated blacks I met at school and the aggressive ones I avoided on the street, it became easy to imagine that the blacks were the ones who had it good in America. This is more than just a harmless childhood fantasy of mine. It is a common, if usually unspoken, belief among whites.

The reason this dumb idea persists is because we are like a biker with the wind so favorable at our backs that we don't even notice our advantage. It is difficult for us to imagine what it must be like—how it must change everything—to be born biking into a head wind. We have become so accustomed to having the wind at our backs, so spoiled by our good fortune, that it seems to us a great injustice that the wind should subside, or switch directions, and blow, even for a minute, in any other way.

Nevertheless, it was their veneer of power, rather than their underlying powerlessness, that attracted me to blacks. I was drawn by admiration rather than pity—this is what separates the white rap fan from the white missionary. I had always had delinquent tendencies, and who could symbolize my wild side better than the bands of boisterous black boys who I and everyone I knew feared? Newspaper columnist Mike Royko once compared housing projects to beehives. Like a lot of boys, I would kill bees, and throw rocks at their hives—not because they had stung me, but because my fear of them became an excuse to unleash my own violence. I felt the same way about blacks in the ghetto. It's lucky I was raised by liberals! I might very well have tried to kill them.

AREN'T YOU IN THE WRONG NEIGHBORHOOD?

The six-flat condo I grew up in was perfectly integrated: two white families, two black, and two mixed. The apartments across the street were home to many black youngsters. Yet even in these harmonious circumstances, whether by parental design, personal preference, or simple habit, my playmates of choice were almost always white. For all my fascination, I knew little of black people. Even in places like Hyde Park, most whites never do.

By age 11, curiosity got the better of me. I joined the neighborhood baseball league, and transferred to Kenwood Academy, a public magnet school. Like most of Hyde Park's public institutions, both were about nine-tenths black. One of my classmates at Kenwood, Mike Davis, went on to become the only white student at Morehouse College. Within a few years, the experiences I had would allow me to outgrow my first layer of naiveté, the one that most white Americans, including most of the whites at Kenwood, don't realize they are still wearing.

Midway through grammar school, I made a discovery. Michael Jackson, Prince, and most of the other rock stars I stood admiring one day in the record store display window, were black. From this massive insight followed others. Practically all of the wittiest, the coolest, the strongest, the most agile, and the most precocious kids I knew were black (in part this was because most of the whites I knew were unusually dull and spoiled). In the locker room, the black boys really did seem to have bigger dicks. Although it has been proven untrue scientifically, you couldn't have told me that at the time. Next to them, my voice was flat, my personality dull, my lifestyle bland, my complexion pallid. I didn't yet know race was the national obsession. I thought obsessing about blacks was, like masturbation, my dirty little secret.

As embarrassing as all of this was, its importance shouldn't be overlooked. The most promising thing about spilled milk is that it has ventured from its container. The most promising thing about the Cool White, the white b-boy, the wannabe (or to update Norman Mailer's term, the white nigga), is that he is defying in some way the circumstances of his birth. He harbors curiosity and admiration for a people his people have stepped on. He lives by his fascinations rather than his habits, his awkwardness rather than his cool. But it is the desire to be cool that drives him. And it is this desire—not only his guilt—that blacks must use to judo some of his power away from him.

My romanticization of blacks was also a way to elevate myself. If blacks were the superior race, then by association, I too was superior. This conceit, shared by all wiggers, is founded on (what seems to us our rare) ability to mingle with blacks who other whites find inaccessible. In fact, we flatter ourselves; fitting in requires no uncommon talent. The main reason more whites don't become wiggers—instead of just white rap fans—is that getting down with blacks, like any relationship, requires that precious, ego-endangering resource: effort.

Effort is why the white b-boy, the wigger, rather than the white liberal, is at the center of my attention. The white liberal is a worthless frustration to black efforts; he has never put any skin on the line and he never will. The white missionary has guts, but he also has his own agenda, whether religious or ideological. The white b-boy, at his best, avoids the drawbacks of both. He has the zeal of the missionary, but he lacks a firm agenda. And unlike both, he knows blacks first as people, not as issues.

How thrilling it was to be the only white kid who knew that "11th and Hamilton" meant the juvenile court and detention center, and knew the calendar number, reputation, and drinking habits of the judges there. How critical it was to understand that "I'm going to kick your white ass" is not so much a threat as a test. How illuminating to eat dinner as a friend in the houses of kids who thought Hyde Park was a place to tease, taunt, and take bikes from white people (especially the ones who did their best to avoid black teenagers).

But I didn't infiltrate black teenage society instantly. Much of my initiation came from the loose-knit bunch of kids at my school who were into hip-hop. Partly popular, partly outcasts, our interracial band of troublemakers grew up on hip-hop together.

Unlike sports or music, the more conventional ports of entry into blackness, hip-hop was a total culture. It involved art, music, sport, risk, media, teenage foolishness, mischief, and an instant citywide network of homeys. For the first year or so, most of my breakdancing and graffiti partners were white, Mexican, or Puerto Rican. By ninth grade, when breakdancing died and most of my white friends, after one or two arrests, had abandoned hip-hop and graffiti for drugs and skateboarding—activities I found dull in comparison—I immersed myself deeper into the city-wide family of graffiti writers, rappers, dancers, DJs, and delinquents.

Imagine what an adventure it must have been for a 13-year-old upper middle-class white kid with overprotective parents to steal and stash cases of spray paint, sneak out at night, travel all over the city (I wonder how white moms in passing cars explained me!), run from the cops, dodge trains in subway tunnels, walk alone through the projects, pick up girls at all-black dances, and commit other crimes for

VICTOR SAVOLAINEN

33

which the statute of limitations has not yet passed. And on top of that, to be accepted by all but the bitterest of the blacks. I was almost instantly and undeservingly made welcome, either directly in the form of: "Brother," "Cool white boy," "That white boy crazy," "You black," "You my nigga," or indirectly, as in "Aren't you in the wrong neighborhood?" or "What (gang) you ride?" etc.—and all the nonverbal comments which meant the same thing.

My favorite of these was told by a white police officer who was writing me up at the 21st district: "Shit. (scribble scribble) I marked down that you were black. You must be the first white kid I've arrested in . . . a long time. Stick with your own kind if you know what I mean." In reply to his mistake, I waited until he had left his office, then mistakenly tore down the anti-graffiti poster hanging on his wall, and shoved it down my pants.

One day my Little League coach arranged for our rag-tag baseball team to scrimmage against a well-trained white suburban team. Warming up, I remember feeling proud to be the only white boy on this black team, and felt certain that our raw city talent would prevail. Within a few innings, we lost by slaughter rule. It was then that I realized for the first time in no uncertain terms that black people did not rule the world.

Experiences like this fed the missionary in me. The small cruelties of elementary school cliques, if not our own families, teach all of us how it feels to be the outcast or the underdog. While some of us spend our lives escaping this feeling, and some inflict the feeling onto others a la Napoleon, others take to the Gandhi role.

What began as a social infatuation with blacks and hip-hop slowly evolved into a political agenda. Sent back to University of Chicago High School sophomore year for bad grades and behavior, I found the social scene so boring and myself so out of place that I turned to loner activities like reading and writing. Frustrated by the inequalities of my two worlds, I gravitated toward what are unappealingly called "political activism" and "community service."

My own need was to be accepted by both worlds, to change them, perhaps to integrate them; but as anyone who's tried it knows, challenging people mainly just alienates them. Whites were the hardest to talk to. For blacks at least, their goal was universally understood: they had to make it in the white world and uplift the race. This was a core value of American society, and one that needed no justification.

But why should whites want to change, to climb down the social ladder—to slay their fears? To brook adventure? To become more worldly? As much as we may admire romantic motives such as these in our heroes (Robinson Crusoe, Tom Sawyer) we look on them as abnormal and suspicious in real life. Most of us would rather play it safe. As my grandmother says: "That's crazy, running around in the gutter with the blacks all night. Why would you want to lower yourself running with the niggers?"

Besides, in heroes all qualities are believed to come effortlessly. The reluctant detective is dragged into the case, dragged into bed with the beautiful client. For most of us, unfortunately, adventure and discovery generally require not just risk, but effort.

Where black people tend to take constructive criticism constructively, and read candor as a sign of respect, whites tend to have the opposite response. Challenge is taken as unfriendly, a threat, something to be avoided. Defensiveness betrays their underlying shame. Even now, when non-hip-hop acquaintances ask me what my favorite kind of music is, I try to avoid the subject. "Everything," I lie.

On matters of race, I naturally found it easier to talk to blacks. As recently as two years ago, I was DJing radio shows and writing under pen-names as though I was black. In one article, I scripted myself as the ghost of Malcolm X who humbles an ego-trippin modern-day black kid for not studying history. Another article I wrote even prompted a white boy from Oxnard, California to mail a whiny letter to the editor, complaining about my anti-white sentiment.

My extreme view had to be tempered with an opposite extreme view: blacks are stupider than whites. I don't recall the first time I thought that, probably pretty early on, and oftentimes I still imagine pseudo-scientifically that it is true. Usually it is based on an observed instance of black stupidity, but I could pretty much rationalize it out of thin air, or even contrary to the facts at hand. My mind wants to believe in hierarchy. I am unable to imagine equality, unable to love blacks without simultaneously hating them. The same mind that believes a dumb black dude has the potential of an Einstein has to restrain itself from shouting "nigger" when he goes to see a brilliant black scholar give a lecture.

All that shit those great racial healers talk about just doesn't click with me inside. It is with this schizophrenic mind that I, and to some degree all, Americans try to forge for ourselves a sensible opinion on race. Usually it doesn't work. One of my first racial causes—imagine this!—was to dismantle black people's stereotypes of *me*. The wind at my back, I actually believed that I was doing black people a favor by showing them I had rhythm. Why couldn't these blacks—the few who wouldn't accept me—wake up and realize that I was down with them?

The main way I expressed my downness, it turned out, was to dis anyone who wasn't as down as I was, especially anyone associated with house music, R&B, the Fresh Prince, anyone at all except for the hardest of hardcore b-boys. Hell, I even dissed them. At age 14, when, as Dres of Black Sheep says, "I dreamt I was *hard*," I initiated a battle with Orko, one of the kings of Chicago graffiti, a quick-witted Jheri-Kurl writer who was not much bigger than me physically, but four years my senior and straight out of jail. The battle turned nasty when I defaced a rooftop with a suggestive message about a certain female family member. "My mama just died!" he shouted when he finally caught up to me, catching me off guard long enough to apply a coat of spray paint to my face. The color he chose, "beige" almost perfectly matched my skin—a sharp reminder that I was not just any graffiti writer, but a white graffiti writer, from a good home, and with a fraction of Orko's problems.

I learned this lesson slowly. It was during a phase when I was trying to analogize the black experience in my own experience. Around the time of the Orko incident, I had changed my graffiti name to Jew 2 and began wearing a Star-of-David medallion. Jews had been oppressed too, hadn't we? And wasn't Israel right next to Africa? My short experiment in contrived cultural chauvinism (being a Jew was not, after all, a big part of my daily life) ended one day after gym class in the Kenwood locker room. I was on friendly, if adversarial, terms with Abnar Farrakhan (son of Minister Louis Farrakhan), one of the coolest, toughest, and most intelligent kids at Kenwood. One day Abnar started talking shit about Jews, basically to get a rise out of me. I called him nigger, basically to get a rise out of his father that night at the dinner table. We got in each other's face and he body-slammed me.

The next summer, community service programs had channeled my aggression into a more enlightened scheme. Instead of battling against black kids, I would educate them—not on math or science, you understand, but on themselves. Their music, their history, their politics, their culture, and their problems, which always fell into three conveniently demonizable categories: racists, sell-outs, and suckers—none of which included me. Like the black who assimilates into the white world, my mission was to blend in and defy the stereotypes of my race. The only difference was, where white culture was built on black people's backs, black culture was built on white people's scraps. I was the president of General Electric mailing his $35 pledge to Greenpeace.

HADN'T I JUST BEEN
A SPECIAL WHITE BOY?

All the while, I was so preoccupied, as all explorers are, with my own experiences that it took a long time to notice some basic insights about how black people see the world. Not that they think as a group, but there are patterns.

I was going deeper into the ghetto, later at night, for longer periods of time, and, more and more frequently, alone. How was I able to do this when in integrated Hyde Park, my own neighborhood, the blacks were already so hostile? Weren't the blacks in my neighborhood just the tip of the iceberg? Weren't blacks in the ghetto far more angry and violent toward whites, just as the whites who lived in all-white neighborhoods would terrorize any black family who tried to move in? Hadn't I just been lucky—a *special* white boy?

For the first few years I thought so. But after a couple of times getting into fights with black dudes in Hyde Park, and the lack of static I encountered in the ghetto, I began to wonder. The only time anyone had ever fucked with me in the ghetto I was waiting for a bus at the 55th/Garfield El station where a lot of whites catch the bus into Hyde Park. It took a long time to occur to me that these guys had fucked with me not because I was in the ghetto, but because it seemed to them that I, like all the other white people who wait at that bus stop, was trying to get away from the ghetto. The whites who do stick around are the poverty pimps—police, landlords, school teachers, and social workers—and only until they pick up their checks.

Where once I found black behavior offensive, I finally began to see that it was in fact *defensive*. This insight was corroborated from another angle when I went to hear Abnar's dad, Minister Louis Farrakhan, give a public speech at the Nation of Islam National Center on 73rd and Stony Island. From a crowd of maybe twenty thousand, not more than five to ten whites. While the people sitting next to me cheered furiously when Farrakhan spoke against the white man, more than one of them—the very same people—made it a point to be friendly to me, shake my hand, and call me "brother". And because I had to leave before the end, the FOI security guard who escorted me to the door put his arm around me and asked me how I liked the speech.

The reason for the apparent paradox was clear. Even the most militant blacks don't hate whites individually just because we're white. They have a double consciousness. They believe, as Farrakhan says, that white folks should be regarded with the same suspicion as snakes: not all of them are bad, but you don't want to go around picking up snakes to try to find a good one. So when someone makes anti-white generalizations, black people know to interpret it correctly as over-statement, the overstatement of someone who is tired of biking into the wind. White people, however, take the rhetoric literally. It becomes their excuse for not bothering to become one of the whites who militant blacks don't hate. For his part, Farrakhan is a moderating force in American race relations. A lot of people are ready to hear something far more extremist than what he's actually saying. He doesn't abuse the demagogue role. We ought to thank our lucky stars he isn't calling for an all-out race war Long Island Rail Road style.

In general, black aggression toward whites is not so much about hating whitey as it is a reaction and an attempt to overcome the humiliation we continue to heap on them. As with any relationship, people need to be met on their own turf, understood on their own terms, and respected for who they are and what they have to offer. To be black is to feel used, unappreciated, condescended to, to be told you are ugly, stupid, abnormal, inferior, violent. This result is accomplished just as effectively by ignoring, avoiding, or patronizing someone—or someone's entire area of the city—as it is

Copyright ©1993 Antek

WIGGERS

through active mistreatment. This is as true in the relationships between the races as it is in the relationship between two people.

Simply because I went alone to hear Minister Farrakhan, because it was in a black neighborhood, because I took the bus, listened carefully, and clapped when I agreed with him (sometimes even when no one else was clapping—okay, I admit that was kind of rude), it seemed to make the people sitting around me think I was pretty okay. Had I gone to see Farrakhan as part of a group, or waited until he was speaking downtown or on a college campus, or had I gone much further in displaying my disagreement with some of what he said, no doubt I would have been received differently.

Yet these are the very circumstances in which most whites encounter anti-white sentiment: not in a black neighborhood, not by themselves, and not with a basic respect for the speaker. It is this invisible sense of turf, along with the wind at our backs, that so few whites perceive the importance of in race relations. This is why so much anti-white sentiment in America is held not by slum dwellers but by successful blacks, educated and living among white people.

But anyone who thinks there is some kind of secret formula to manipulate and get accepted by blacks is sure to be disappointed. Black people will see through you and, more than likely, they'll snicker about you later, or call your bluff outright if they're feeling courageous—oftentimes, even where you are most convinced of your own sincerity. Earning the trust of a wide range of blacks—not just the friendly and servile ones—means turning your world upside down. And that's on top of taking risks, having good intentions, commitment, a sincere interest, and an open mind. It's a weeding out process that few of us understand, much less get very far with. Perhaps it is comparable, in a small way, to the initiation process of blacks into white society.

The most common way whites seek to become initiated—by having black friends or a black-oriented talent—are by themselves flimsy. When asked why he didn't venture into Harlem, an aspiring white rapper from lower Manhattan said he was going to wait until "I get famous and people know who I am, then it'll be cool." Whites who don't need costumes or gimmicks or hip-hop to hang out with blacks do so because they put black people at ease, not by some superficial trick, but because our basic respect for and familiarity with their culture shines through in all the subtle ways that you can only understand from experience. Learning about black culture at a distance (through music and books) may be even worse than not learning about it at all. Most of the time, we use our knowledge of blacks and their culture as we have always used it, to manipulate them, rather than to repair our own sick habits.

Just because I have gone further than most whites does not mean I belong to some special category, deserving to be judged as anything other than the white boy I am. I was, after all, born biking with my back to the wind. If after eleven years, I decide to swing a U and retrace my path going into the wind for awhile just to see what it's like, it does little to even my personal score. For a long time I denied this, creating an intricate mythology about just how down I was. If you've been reading carefully, you've noticed that I still have that impulse.

But at least now I think I've pretty much come to terms with what my place is. Rather than posturing about the pros and cons of affirmative action as a government policy, I make it my personal policy. Rather than waving signs, "fighting racism" and attacking "sellouts," I merely spend money in black-owned businesses and work for real-life causes such as the careers of my black friends. I no longer need to dress as a b-boy. Unlike two of my close white friends, I have not become a rapper. Rather than writing as though I myself am black, I work collaboratively with black writers. It took a long time for me to begin to comprehend what Tarek Thorns, my classmate at Oberlin College, refers to as not stepping in people's "cultural space".

American white boys like me have our own space. It's a pretty nice space too. We live somewhere that books like this are available, people have the training to comprehend them, the excess mental energy to think about them, and the luxury to act on them. Keeping in mind that the average earthling survives on less than $2000 per year, I consider myself pretty lucky. Unhampered by bad health, perilous psychological hang-ups, immediate violence, money hardships, etc. I am able, more so than ninety-nine percent of the world's people, to do what I want to in life.

This happy circumstance for me is neither something to feel guilty about nor to take for granted. It is a rare something that has happened to me, in an important sense because of the misfortune of others, and relies on my continuing ability to exploit my advantage over them. That is the reason why I am getting paid to write about hip-hop, while the people who taught me about hip-hop are in jail, dead, or strugglin, scramblin 'n' gamblin. This is neither something to fight, nor to gloat about, nor to sit back and be thankful over. It is merely a moral debt. There are many moral debts in the world, and one of mine belongs to black America, with some individuals bigger creditors than others. This is not a burden, something to get all martyred out about, and it is not a joke. It is merely an opinion. If I never repay black America in my lifetime, I will have gone unpunished for a permanent theft.

So what is the proper place of whites? I've been toying with this question for more than a decade now, yet I am still so far from being a model white person (as far as I'm concerned, even if such a description is proper, I've yet to meet one who can fill it). I still have a lot more to learn from blacks. I still have irrational fears of them. I still slip into degrading white ways of seeing (one of the worst of these is when I don't expect enough from them). My speech and attitude still slip into caricature and invasions of their cultural space. (They'll be happier to share their culture with us when we begin sharing our spoils, instead of always trying to take, then denying we have taken, what's theirs.) By learning more from them than I give back, I am still accruing a deficit every year on top of the towering debt I already owe.

Like the black trying to make it in white America, we face a catch-22: We cannot help blacks without undercutting their self-determination; we cannot be cool without encroaching on their cultural space; we cannot take risks without exercising our privilege to take risks; we cannot integrate without invading; we cannot communicate on black terms without patronizing.

Faced with these choices, we need not become paralyzed. Instead we may follow the example of blacks who cross-over in the opposite direction: develop a double consciousness. We must take the risks necessary to do right, yet we must remain sober in recognizing that, unlike blacks trying to make it in white America, our struggle is not the center of importance.

Someone like me takes race so seriously, some have wondered, how can I proceed through life without becoming paralyzed by a million depressing moral dilemmas?

In a land that James Baldwin once described as "dedicated to the death of the paradox," we remain at war with life's indivisible contradictions, unappreciative of their richness. "I'm confused about what your point of view is," an editor of mine once said. "I can't tell from reading this whether you are a hip-hopper or a racist, an insider in black society, or some kind of outside sociologist. Do you like black people or do you hate them?" My answer is that I'm human, meaning that I'm complex enough to be all of these things at once.

If only black people could get away with that.

A JOB OPENING IN CLEVELAND

The last time I wanted to bomb this bad, I probably had a lollipop in my mouth. Back in the mid '80s, back in Chicago, back when I was an eager young toy and every new name on a mailbox was my potential pen pal—now all I see on the mailbox is another six-lollipop sucker with a five letter name who writes four different three-letter crews on a two-year mission to hit spots once they've already been hit, invent nothing, inspire no one, and then zip. The last time I wanted to go bombing that bad, I was one of those very suckers.

And even then I was dreaming about Cleveland. I had seen on a map that it was the only other midwestern city with train lines (St. Louis just got theirs last year). It *had* to have graffiti. (Then again, so'd Montreal . . .)

As far as I knew, the only graffiti Cleveland ever produced was that crooked, bubble-letter, "Wizard" piece in *Spray Can Art* which didn't even deserve to be in there because where were Boston, Connecticut, Baltimore, Miami, New Orleans, San Diego, Portland, Seattle, or any of the two-bit towns that could burst Mr. Wizard's bubble and send him farting down the fire escape.

Isolation had allowed Chicago hip-hop to maintain an '80s sensibility while the coasts were overrun with that trendy shit (Like my friend Al says: "These new-school rhymes when suckers speakin double-time too confusin. It's losin somethin in the translation."). Cleveland's even more isolated than Chicago. Could Cleveland be a miniature Chicago, or did Cleveland's underground shrivel up during the dry years following the official death of breakdancing?

Noon on a Saturday in late summer, I board an orange and silver RTA train into Cleveland from the airport on the far West Side. It looks like a trolley because they're only running one car. Aside from a faded tag on one of the cushion seats, there are no signs of graffiti.

If there are any graffiti writers here, they haven't discovered scratch-bombing. I like this place already.

The train rushes quietly along the Red Line toward downtown. There are two other lines; they go to the suburbs. Passengers are eyeing me nervously because I've got this big bag of spray paint and I'm standing in the aisle getting whiplash trying to look out the windows at all the walls. There are SO many walls. The Red Line runs alongside freight tracks (Conrail, for all you freight bombers). At first we're slightly elevated, passing factory walls; toward downtown, we dip into open-roofed train valleys with walls on both sides. Then we arc over this big spectacular bridge and we slide underneath a building at the foot of a modest skyline. We emerge on the East Side. More walls. Viaduct walls, factory walls. WALLS.

I am Captain Kirk investigating a foreign planet for signs of intelligent life. Approximately one hundred pieces sighted. Most of them are faded and disappointingly Wizard-like, one-shot attempts from the breakin days. Maybe twenty show decent style. Four, maybe five, look recent. One has a neat-capped "Los Angeles" next to it.

Also sighted: one throw-up; this makes me happy. Hardly any tags. Fewer tags than pieces! This also makes me unspeakably happy. An enterprising bomber could take King of Cleveland by walking the tracks one night. Trains stop running at 2 am. Almost none of the walls look buffed. Electricity runs overhead; there are no third rails! The only thing to watch out for is Mister Probation camping out in the stations.

I'm not even going to talk about the train yards. Yes, they're easy, but you're not allowed to bomb them as a personal favor to me. Cleveland is struggling not to become another Detroit and scare all its capital off to the suburbs. If you're going to do graffiti in Cleveland, do it to help Cleveland back up, not to kick it while it's down.

On the East Side, I am the only white passenger; shorties down the aisle are saying some rhymes from off the radio. They know someone who writes graffiti they say, but they won't tell me where he lives.

"You look like a cop. You look like a 21 Jumpstreet." This is the oldest speaking.

I show them my spray paint.

"Fine, but you can't come around our neighborhood. Only the strong survive around there."

"Just tell me where to get off," I say.

"Get off with us," the youngest one finally answers.

"Don't try to follow us, man," says only the strong survive.

East Cleveland: End of the Line. I walk all over looking for clues. In half an hour I see two tags on a grocery store; character outlines in a viaduct. Big ol piece on the side of a building: awkward gray bell-bottomed letters "J-Roc R.I.P." with a tombstone, a blue cloud, and no signature. It kind of redefined the whole neighborhood. Imagine saying that about a piece in New York.

On Euclid Avenue—their 125th Street—a dude named Jay is air-brushing T-shirts at a neighborhood festival. His boy is spinning on the 1s and 2s and an MC gets on the open mic. (An MC at my college tells me Cleveland has some underground talent. It is definitely boycotting this occasion.) Jay is a nice guy though. He doesn't have anything up on the line but he's gone bombing a few times and tells the stories with great drama. "Did you see where they tore down that factory? We used to have our pieces up there. Yeah we were out one night and a helicopter chased us. We just ran inside the building but the police never came. It's hard to tag around here—did you see that tag under the viaduct? Yeah, that was nothin. The only way we got to do that was when the power went out. I went up there with spray paint. All I had was that can of white. People don't really get into graffiti that much around here. Half of them don't even know what it is."

Do you know any other writers?

"There's someone writing DNA. He writes it everywhere."

Where does he stay at?

"I don't know. I wish I could meet him. Somewhere around here."

I ask Jay if he wants to come piecing tonight. He says he'll see and gives me his card. I get back on the line to scope out my walls. Second time around on the West Side, I catch one of the names: Rox One 113. Rox has his name next to four or five faded little pieces in between 70th and 120th streets. 21 Jumpstreet in effect. I go looking for his ass.

117th and Madison Station, factory district. In an alley on 112th, one of Rox's faded old tags has been traced over in fresh white chalk. The next alley is bingo. There are like ten wack pieces on garages, but it doesn't matter that they're wack because I am so fucking geeked to see them. A yardful of dirty little blond kids with beer bottles is watching me and this bad little 10-year-old girl comes over to flirt. Her little brother offers me one of the beer bottles, which are filled with water. The guy who does graffiti is named Mike and he lives three houses down, they tell me. He has curly blond hair too.

"Hi, I'm Upski," I say. "I'm a writer from Chicago."

Rox One and his boy Presto flip out. Rox One is wearing a

Grateful Dead t-shirt and his favorite adjective is "killer." "Killer . . . Killer . . ." The more you get to know him, the more you get to hear him say it. Rox One and Presto chill with me all day, apologizing for all these old pieces around their neighborhood. Presto who is sort of a mentor to Rox, has an airbrush store and a skilled, imaginative piecebook. He draws weird, gory characters that he isn't sure he could put up on a wall, and all his sentences start out "In Cleveland, see..." Neither of them have been caught before, but they're paranoid all the same. Presto keeps asking me if I'm sure I'm not a cop.

21 Jumpstreet. Freeze Mothafuckas!

"I'm serious," he says. "In Cleveland, there are so few writers that the police can just track you down—just like you did."

Is that why graffiti died in Cleveland?

"It didn't ever die really. There are a lot of writers out there. A lot of Hispanics at my high school did it. It just never happened, I guess you could say. Cleveland just got a bad name from that Wizard shit in *Spray Can Art*. There was shit up on the lines in the early '80s that was better than that Wizard shit. Sometimes people from Pittsburgh come here and do shit just to rub our faces in it that we aren't doing shit."

"Come piecing with me tonight," I say.

Rox hasn't gone piecing in two years. Presto hasn't gone in four. They look at each other. "We could do something in the alley," they suggest.

Fuck that, I say. I didn't come all the way to Cleveland to paint in an alley. They look at each other again. They're having trouble thinking of a wall on the line, but Rox finally remembers one. It gets late. We follow a little trail through the bushes and come out by this beautiful primed wall. It's like ten feet from the tracks. We do a quick piece and I walk them home. They might start piecing again, they say.

Temporarily homeless, I decide to sleep up on the tracks next to our piece. I fall asleep and dream about turning Cleveland into a graffiti paradise. But I don't have a lollipop in my mouth anymore. I am an adult now, and my vision of graffiti has grown up too. In the dream there is no scratch-bombing, no tagging, no throw-ups, or even individual pieces. I organize all the local graffiti writers, and we map out the walls on the line; then we design and paint every single wall, one by one, top to bottom, end to end, a three-hundred block long art gallery.

A single, unified masterpiece chopped up into hundreds of masterful pieces: Something so beautiful it would remake Cleveland and all the little kids would get geeked and ridiculous, and start to break and freestyle and stop killing each other and all the jobs from the suburbs would move back into the city and everyone from Chicago would move there too. And the Mayor of Chicago would get mad and say "Damn, where is all my citizens at?" and then he'd call me and say I had to come back to Chicago because we didn't have no more citizens . . .

And then it was light out and I woke up and looked at our piece. I saw how wack it was. I took that as a sign that I don't have the talent or attention span for a job like that. If you do, I think the position's still open. Go to Cleveland and apply in person. **(1993)**

MESSAGE TO MARIO: WEAR YOUR MASK

We used to have a joke that spray paint was fucking up our memories. A few weeks ago, Mario called me with a new joke. When we were 13 and 14, we painted dozens of walls together, traded girls, fought gang-bangers, battled other crews, and talked on the phone almost every day. For a while, Mario was my best friend. After we stopped hanging out, he got even deeper into painting. He painted with different partners every week, traded photos around the world, and filled his life with graffiti. Even the great Trixter had said he was a graffiti head.

We used to have a joke that spray paint was fucking up our memories. A few weeks ago Mario called me with a new joke. "It wasn't the memory, it was the bladder," he said. "About a year ago I started noticing I had to use the washroom more often. Before I learned to control it, I would urinate in bed even. It kept getting worse. Now, I can't drink anything for two hours before I go to bed. I pee once before bed, then I have to get up twice during the night."

The neurotoxins in spray paint have damaged the part of Mario's brain which produces hormones to control his bladder. The label on any spray can will tell you it can also damage the immune and nervous system, kidney, liver and lungs—the same is true for a lot of markers.

Anyone who's gone piecing has felt the slight dizziness and loss of appetite. Some of us get headaches and nausea. I personally get muscle spasms and my hair is starting to go (one of four graffiti writers I know who're balding early). In the long run, who knows? Spray

paint could be our asbestos, our AIDS.

Coincidentally, I have a second friend named Mario. This Mario lives on the West Side, and he's at least as much of a graffiti head as the first Mario. He paints at least as much as the first Mario, and has at least as many problems. "All my life, I never used to pick my nose," he told me recently. "Then in 1988, I started having to pick my nose all the time, getting paint-colored snot, scratchy throat, wheezing. Then one time, I did this real big production and I coughed up blood. After that I lost my voice for like a week. Dude, I was scared. I didn't want anybody to know. The doctor told me don't spray paint no more. I kept doing it, and my symptoms kept getting worse. I stutter . . . I get a tightness in my eye, twitches in my wrist . . . Dude, I get major, major headaches . . . The worst part is, I feel like I'm getting stupider; I can't articulate myself as well as I used to be able to . . . I think I'm addicted to doing graffiti, I fiend for it. Graffiti is my life. I feel like I might have to die for it."

I have to admit, death by graffiti sounds like an honorable way to go out. I dream of it myself. But isn't that giving up at the game, copping out at the challenge of life: the challenge to be stronger, smarter, healthier, better than we thought we could be. The challenge to survive.

Mario, I don't want to visit you in the hospital or the cemetery, and I don't want you to visit me there. Sometime in life, I too may have to cough up blood, to lose my hair, or to lose my mind because of the painting I've done. But I ain't going out like no sucker.

When I use spray paint, I do everything to dilute the toxins and keep them out of my body. I eat before and after painting, use the wind to avoid inhaling fumes, steer clear of other toxins, refuse to paint indoors, and refuse to go out unless I really care about the piece. Most of all, I wear gloves and a mask, changing the filters regularly. I'm wearing that fucker right now. Please wear your mask too, Mario. Both of you. That shit ain't funny no more.

OUT OVER THE STAIRWELL

I had a dream last night that I was running desperately through an El station, pursued by Lt. Arnold Schwarzenegger, the newest member of the Chicago graf squad. He'd been gaining on me for blocks. I've given him a tour of the urban obstacle course, and now I gots to give it to him: the motherfucker's faster than me (like I said, it was a dream). As we reach the top of a staircase, he is reaching for my shoulder. Suddenly, I snap to the floor, brace myself, and say farewell as I launch him out over the stairwell.

Just thinking about this thrills me. Not because I want to pay him back for all the bad movies he's made, or because I made up a clever rhyme scheme (it was really made up by Art of Origin: "Say farewell as I kick you down the stairwell"). It's the *physics* of the thought that thrills me, the trajectory of his body, tripped from a sprint, hang-gliding headlong and helpless. The sublime use of space.

Graffiti taught me all I know about space. Back in '86, Scrawl Master Scarce had an empire of space. On a crowded bus, his hand would wander out the window momentarily and a perfect "SMS" would appear in Griffin above the pane on the outside.

Talk about space, I heard of a writer who dollied his boy around downtown in a refrigerator box. The box was dollied up against a wall then dollied away, revealing two carefully crafted tags. I liked the box trick. My interpretation was to set it along the catwalk next to those "nowhere to hide when the train comes" walls. Then I would hide in the box and piece all night while trains roared past my head. (I was hiding elsewhere that time the train decided to snag my box on something and beat it down the catwalk for half a block against the guard rails before flicking what remained of it—and my paint—out over the alley below.)

When writers don't use space effectively, graffiti loses its appeal. When streets gag on tags and throw up on throw ups, when wildstyles stagnate, graffiti settles into the surrounding scenery. It isn't fresh anymore, no matter how illegal, but stiff with orthodoxy. The continuing vitality of graffiti depends in part on whether we can continue to surprise with the use of space.

DEAR STEVEN: HIP-HOP IS NOT A WAY OF LIFE

We were all hanging out one day last fall, driving around these abandoned buildings to look at some walls. The kid sitting next to me, Steven, was just getting into hip-hop and he loved it with the eagerness of a 12-year-old, although he was 18. He said a couple of bright things that day so I took down his address, and the next week when I mailed out a manuscript for comments, I addressed a copy to Steven. A lot of my best friends didn't write me back, but Steven wrote me back the same day, five pages of scribble-scrabble, not especially well-crafted, but he was eager to learn. We began going to hip-hop meetings together, to breakdancing practice, and to the library. Over the last months, while on probation for graffiti, he's been teaching himself how to beatbox, draw characters, and write. So far, he has written a few stories which have been published in small hip-hop magazines. Here is one of my favorite:

THIS IS A WARNING!!!

'93 is over and it's time to let the shit hit the fan. You city jerks (I mean workers) and Grand Wizard Daley, this is a warning: You have one month to clear out your stupid, senseless anti-graffiti programs, rent-a-cops (graf squad) and K-9 who stand in the middle of the aisles like big-ass overseers thinking they can't get their ass kicked. Your mutt tries to get near me while I'm painting, Fido is on the tracks. In October, you iced our Wall of Fame, now you have to pay the price. You gumps have taken this power thing too far, now it's time to show you who really has the damn power in this city.

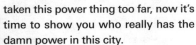

With a flash of the Krylon emergency symbol, writers from Philly, New York, Atlanta, and Cali will be here in minutes through the secret subway, where trains never get buffed and city jerks (administrators) get hung from abandoned trains with fat laces . . . Where graffiti squad cops get treated like a pig: Pumped full of chemicals and fried like bacon at a truck stop.

We do want to thank you money swindling devils for two things: The electricity that comes through the connecting wires from most of your homes and the paint we re-confiscated from 39th and Michigan. We simply let one of our stoolies in your Human Resources department take a 14% deduction from your paycheck; you thought you were getting a pay cut from taking the day off to play booty with yourselves. Perverts. Sit on your ass, don't do shit and we'll be running the city like the rats and roaches. Think about it the next time you open up a new line. Every night, me and my crew can go out and cold wreck 9-5 yards, Howard Yards, Wilson Yards and not even have to worry about you sneaking up on us. If you try something stupid, we'll assign all of our city workers, Guardian Angels (G.A. aka Graffiti Alliance) and clumsy broken-down-ass graffiti blasters (retired salt trucks with a big douche bottle on top) to paint and bomb up the whole city. Graffiti Alliance is responsible for graffiti on

HARRISON WILLIAMS

WRITERS

the North and South Side lines. You didn't think about patting them down and checking them for gear, did you? Bumble-fucks! You didn't even bother checking the buttons on their hats, which turn out to be a gold spray paint can. Why do you think they have a picture of a train line on their "Join Us And Be A Hero Like Me" advertisement plugger.

We got them on our side and damn skippy we'll use them. It's up to you city administratin' fools. One month to get your shit together and scrape off the Wall of Fame, or feel the wrath of HIP-HOP. YOU SUCKERS!!!

Dear Steven,

I found an old phone book the other day. From 1988—it wasn't even old. In it, I counted 127 names of MCs, b-boys, DJs and writers whose phone numbers I had at the time. And these were only the ones with phones! These were the hip-hoppers that time forgot. Former MC giants on the chicken-bone circuit, kings of the line, masters of the linoleum . . . okay, there were a few suckers in there too. But of those 127 people, only 23 remain active in hip-hop today (less than one in five).

If I go back a little further to 1984–85, the demographics get even bleaker. That was when I first started out in the neighborhood, before I went all-city. I probably knew 40 or 50 other kids who were into hip-hop. These were my mentors, my partners, the ones who swore they'd be hip-hop forever. *One* of them is left. That's Deep UFG-THC.

If old-schoolers (middle-schoolers in my case) know anything, we know what it's like to be abandoned, to think hip-hop is dying and to keep doing it anyway. That's why we don't take new-schoolers seriously. We've seen too many of you fall off. As my old friend K-Lite said: Sometimes I look at myself in the mirror and I feel like I'm a unicorn—I feel like I'm doing this all alone. It was 1989 when K-Lite said this to me—the height of Chicago's hip-hop drought—and I vowed to myself I would stay in it forever. The next year, K-Lite recorded a song with the rock group Ministry where he shouts things like: You a sucka . . . Wake up . . . And ya don't stop . . . Word. After that, I saw him maybe once. So long for gevity.

When I look at the crew I used to run with in 7th and 8th

grade, it's so terrible what happened to us. The white boys in the crew mostly went off to college. Benj went to Stanford; Prashant the Indian kid went to Cornell. Alan, Seth, and Enemy slipped into drugs, but now they're cleaning up and going off to college too.

The black and Puerto Rican boys in the crew did not go to college. Last I heard, Joe Iglesias is in jail for shooting gangbangers and running a crack house. Michael DeMunster for stealing a car. Salahdin fell off the fire escape. Fest was charged with shooting the road manager of Boyz II Men (he was cleared). Hip-hop, it turned out, was only a temporary bridge between us. When hip-hop wasn't there any more, we returned to our respective sides of the bridge. I look back on the crazy times we had together and it all seems like a lie.

You are from the other side of the bridge, Steven. I don't want my friendship with you to be a lie. You've been into hip-hop for a year now, and are expecting a baby in the fall. If you want to stay into hip-hop, and lead a happy, productive life, you have a very hard battle ahead of you. Especially with how old you are. Most people quit hip-hop by the time they're you're age. It usually goes in three or four year cycles. You get into it when you're about 14. By the time you're 18, you either have to make a career out of it, kick it down to the level of hobby, or quit. That may sound like selling out to you, but which is worse: selling out hip-hop, or selling out *your life* to basic training and Burger King?

You can tell a lot by looking at the old-schoolers who've managed to stay into hip-hop. Trixter customizes cars. Jesse and Slang have stores. Defski makes films. Cashus D teaches. Crunch does community organizing. P-Lee works for Oprah. Him and Stane make records. Reg Noc makes Sprite commercials. D-Zine sells canvases. Fess, Spike, Crack, Crush, Artistic, Riot, Warp, and Rafa airbrush. Kingdom manages. B-boy B does animation. Zore gets grants. Raven gets A's at DePaul. Almost all of them made careers around the talents they learned in hip-hop.

You will hear people say hip-hop is a culture, a way of life. Don't listen to those people. They are usually the first ones who have to quit. Hip-hop is only a way of life when you're in high school. Then you have to make a living. Hip-hop isn't gonna pay your rent. Hip-hop isn't gonna pay your grocery bill, your electric bill; hip-hop doesn't stop bullets; hip-hop doesn't put a marriage back together or regulate a corporation or change a government policy. It doesn't do most of the things we need a culture or a way of life to do for us. That's why I wasn't surprised to hear that my old buddy Secret flipped from being a graffiti writer to a drug dealer to a K-9 security guard assigned to catch graffiti writers. We can tell him fuck you, but we can't give him a real alternative. Hip-hop is only an art. It's only a group of friends. It's only a hobby.

Hip-hop does deserve credit for one thing in your life Steven: getting you into the world of people with promising futures. But hip-hop itself is only a bridge into that world. Your challenge is not so much to climb to the top of the bridge (your punk ass already got me faded in breakin), your challenge is to cross to the other side.

Steven called me yesterday. "I think Chicago hip-hop is getting ready for another drought," he said.

"When? Now?"

"Yeah, things are slowing down. It's been four years. The first cycle was 1984 to 1987, right? This is 1991 to 1994. That's four years."

IF GRAFFITI WAS RAP . . .

If the graffiti I did in 7th and 8th grade was written down as a rap, the first verse would go something like this: "Upski / Upski / Upski / Upski / Up / Upski / Upski / Upski / Up / Up / Upski"

Clever, isn't it? And that was just the Tag Verse. Wait till you see the Piece Verse. It would have more of an: "Upski / *Up* / **UPSKI** / **UP** / Up One / Upski / **Up** / *Upski* / Upski / UPSKI!"

You know what I'm sayin?

Now don't get me wrong. What writers lack in literacy, we make up for in risk. Just how often do you see an MC paying his rhyming dues where we pay ours: on the train lines and streets? Rapping only in studios, on stages, and in ciphers as most MCs do, is like piecing only in piecebooks, permission spots, and sissy-ass wall of fames where only those who already care about your art get to pass judgment.

And imagine writers criticizing a piece because we couldn't read or understand it—like how people said Tung Twista's shit was too fast: That's *lyrical wildstyle* you gumps! So in some ways graffiti is ahead of rap.

But on the verbal side, graffiti is stuck. I'm not saying we all have to run out there and become some kind of Busta Writes or Kool G Rustoleum. A lot of us don't feel we have that much to say (verbally at least) besides name and crew, name and crew, name and crew.

Or if we do write something, it's either—
A. CERTIFIED HIP-HOP SLANG: "Git da fuck off my wall!"
B. A POLITICALLY CONSCIOUS MESSAGE: "Free South Africa" that Lupo would write.
C. DEEPLY MEANINGFUL: like the dedication me and Ages once wrote next to a piece we did for a fallen friend: "The past is done. The future beckons . . ."

Puh-lease!

What makes it worse, a lot of the ones doing this are rappers. Lyricists. "When we used to tag up on trains and in high places, I'd just write Nas or Kid Wave," recalls Nas in an interview for *Rappages*. "I wanted to write riddles and rhymes and make it mean something, but niggas would say we didn't have time for that."

But having all the time in the world to do fill-ins and throw-ups!

How long can we keep calling ourselves graffiti *writers* and not living up to the name?

DEAR KOZAK:
THE RULES OF GRAFFITI *

Scattered in among the fuck-you mail I got from white kids for "We Use Words Like Mackadocious" were half a dozen thoughtful, cre-

---

* Not *the* rules of graffiti. My rules of graffiti. All the clever parts were boosted from and are Copyright © 1993 by Steve Powers in *On the Go #7*.

ANTCK

WRITERS

ative letters that tried to offer solutions to the problems raised. One of these in particular was marked by great clarity and insight. It was a furiously scrawled letter with lots of crossed out words. The writer was 14-year-old Eric Kozak from a small town called Parker, Colorado. I wrote to Eric during the summer of '93 and we began corresponding. He splits his time between his mom's house in Parker (just outside of Denver) and his dad's in Topeka. He is trying to teach himself graffiti, and become a part of hip-hop as best he can under the circumstances.

Dear Kozak,

Cavemen did it, so did Romans and Egyptians. The Incas did it, so did Greeks and Native Americans. There was graffiti on the New York Subway a year after it was built. There's graffiti on the moon. If graffiti is vandalism, and vandalism is garbage, then man has left his mark with garbage all over the universe. So you, with your pathetic desire to be remembered, are in good company. The development of modern graffiti is too long to go into, so go ask your local expert and he'll tell you his version.

Applying paint to a surface illegally is not in itself immoral. Many surfaces such as lamp posts, viaduct walls, or dark rooms deep inside a subway tunnel aren't actually "damaged" by applying paint to them. Laws don't always make sense but anyone who disobeys the law should be prepared to face the consequences, including the possibility that the police will break the law to catch you. When caught, never let them punk you or sweet-talk you into a confession, even if it seems like they already have all the evidence they need. If they had all the evidence they needed, why would they be talking to you? Never for any reason give them any information about any other writers. Snitches and shit-talkers get stitches and need walkers.

Although being a new jack seems undesirable in any hip-hop art form, you should enjoy it while you can. At this stage you can bite all you want with no remorse. All your elders will say is, "Aw, isn't that sweet, kootchie kootchie koo." So steal that freeze, rob that rhyme scheme, and loot whole letterforms. Don't worry about giving any credit, we'll pat ourselves on the back and brag how we're influencing the next generation. But style isn't a crutch or a schtick. It is understanding why the connection you bit flows or why the baseline you boosted bumps. Style is the process to an appealing end. Once you've studied it, you can reinvent your own style. Pretty soon, somebody will steal your secret sauce and the cycle will be renewed.

You may be good, but you're not that good. Keep your fat head to a reasonable swell and get back to work. Soon you'll be able to get a grip on your self-esteem and we'll all be better for it.

Too often, graffiti has become boring, conventional, irrelevant, and at its worst has contributed to the degradation of public transportation and of public life in the city. Too often, it becomes yet another incentive for people to ditch the city, crippling its tax base (which funds schools, hospitals . . .), and giving up on the ideal of America (not that it has ever seriously been followed) as a place where people from different backgrounds

can come together for mutual benefit. Therefore, we strive to elevate our art in three respects: content, location, and process.

Content

1. You suck until further notice.

2. It's gonna take a long time before we even acknowledge your existence, even longer before we can bear to look at that foul scribble you call your name. To speed the process, choose a clever name that means something to you, or defies the norm of simpleminded slang.

Strive to be original—not for its own sake, but because no one has seen things before in precisely the way you see them. Collaborate with MCs and writers to bring their words to the public. Five years from now, most of your work will be gone and forgotten. You might be too. So while you and it are here, make it as memorable as you can. Don't waste time or paint doing fill-ins and throw-ups. Always put up your best stuff first. Don't save it. You could invent a whole new style, or have your eyes poked out, any day now.

Location

Choose spots that maximize the good impact of the work while minimizing its bad side-effects. Maximize public exposure, surprisingness and daring of a piece while minimizing its insult and cost to people of the city. The best targets for piecing are usually abandoned buildings, rooftops, and neighborhood permission walls, especially in unexpected places. Questionable targets include all public or private property that gets buffed and raises the cost of urban living. Racking from stores in the city is questionable too for the same reason.

Then again, you do live in Parker, Colorado.

Also questionable are halls of fame and practice walls where graffiti loses its public importance and adventurousness. The worst targets are those which in addition to the cost of buffing have added bad effects. Bombing windows blocks peoples' view. Bombing houses and stores in the ghetto burdens people who have enough burdens already. The best places to bomb are rich areas, especially rich suburbs.

Try to find fresh walls. Where possible, avoid going over other graffiti. Never go over anything by a dead writer unless he was your friend and out of respect you decide to re-trace his piece for him to restore it. Pieces go over tags and throw-ups. Tags and throw-ups never go over pieces, not even over the background, not even in a war. Avoid piecing over pieces, especially the beautiful or historic. There are too many walls to be doing that. Only go over a piece with a better one, and only if you have a good reason, and ask permission first if possible.

If you do a permission wall, it should either be because you need the money or because you have something you really want to express at that location. Most people who seem like they're being nice by giving you permission walls are really exploiting the hell out of you.

Process

The process of graffiti should link its technical aspects to a greater hip-hop vision. Cleverness and risk are prized. Creative use of space is prized. Ambitiousness is prized. Care should be taken to match the piece with the wall, to paint the whole wall, or to unite multiple walls in series. The writer should constantly ask himself: Who exactly is my audience and how can I possibly move them?

DEEP

An interview with Lesley Thomas
CONFESSIONS OF A SUPER-GROUPIE

"I'd like to send this out to the one the L-E-S / Got a lot of rhythm and style and finesse / Come here love hot sex on da plat / And when ya done wit dat just clap."

—Q-TIP, A TRIBE CALLED QUEST

Lesley, what kind of a kid were you?

LESLEY: Spoiled rotten. I got everything I wanted. My mother worked twenty hours a day. She was a key puncher. She would put Christmas toys on layaway in April. But I didn't know any of that then. For years, I can't remember her kissing and hugging me, but I know she loved me. Me and my little sister De-De stayed in the house by ourself from the time I was like seven, off and on. She'd give us instructions for the next day. The gas-man's gonna come. I would be cookin and talkin on the phone. I was constantly inventing something. I would cut up my mother's outfits. I cut up so many of her outfits until I got my ass beat. I would make a skirt out of a pillowcase and wear it to school.

Yeaa, that's hip-hop.

I was always tryna get everyone's attention. My house was like party central. I never had a curfew. I was out 'till 2 in the morning. In pictures, I was always the one in the middle of the circle acting a fool. I would bogart my way into it, like pushing the birthday girl out of the picture and shit. I was always stealing the spotlight. Always an A student. My teachers were furious. They would always call home. Lesley

JOURNALISTS

will not shut up. She finishes her work before everyone else. Then she talks and all the other kids can't do their work.

I spent most of my life being a bully. I'm just starting to realize this. I'm perceptive. I can see people's weaknesses and people's potential. I kind of had everybody trapped in these circles like a puppeteer. They don't particularly care for me now. By 9th grade, I started getting bored.

Of what?
People. Everything. School. Family. You know how teenagers think they know everything. It seemed like everyone was weak. They couldn't push past their weaknesses. I could tell as much as my teachers. I was like wait a minute. These people are stupid. My uncle Gerry would give me books. I read *The Autobiography of Malcolm X* when I was 11. I knew all this stuff in school was lies, but instead of going against the system, I just didn't go to school. I did the whole party scene. Fake ID. Going into clubs. I would go and do the craziest shit. I would call my mother to come pick me up from a hotel 'cause this guy wanted to have sex. I moved out when I was 15. I hadn't gone to school in like a month. I moved in with this girl named April who was like 20 who had her own apartment. I'd just sit around smoking Newports all day while she went to work.

One day we were sitting around cracking jokes and I cracked a joke on this one girl and got her good. Everybody was laughing for like ten minutes. Then she said, Well at least I got a high school diploma. The next day I called my mother to come and get me.

So then I was a year behind, supposedly. I went to night school. Summer school. I was at this new high school and I just caught rec again. Most popular. Walk out of class. Come back take my test and get an A. Breezed through all that. I had this boyfriend who was a drug dealer. He made a whole lot of money. I would come to school with Gucci, Louie. I took a cab to school any day he didn't pick me up. I would walk around with $400-500 dollars in my pocket he would give me. Everybody was jealous. Teachers, everybody. I was still bored. I was like This bitch ain't gon tell me I can't get no high school diploma. I'll get it like *that*.

My family was like You wanna prove somethin? Go to college. I went to Highland Park Community College. That's where I met Dr. Salsman, the guy who changed my whole thing. He picked up on the challenge thing. He saw the little kid who was always bum-rushing the spotlight and he instigated me. He turned me into like a monster, an academic snob. I would be at school until 10 or 11 at night, just sitting with him talking. I couldn't sleep 'cause I wanted to go to school. Party? Tuh! I couldn't get enough learning.

I lost all my friends. They started calling me dictionary-breath. All the Gucci stuff, that's gone. I sold it. I gave it all away. I went from riding around in a Mercedes to catching the bus, which is a no-no in Detroit. I have friends that don't have jobs because they can't get on the bus. This is the Motor City. How we gonna be on the bus? My boyfriend, I quit him. He didn't understand why. He was gonna keep me from going to this next level.

This admissions officer came one day and gave this big speech about Oberlin. Offering these incredible $20,000 scholarships. I walked out. Dr. Salsman came after me furious. He showed me passages about Oberlin in DuBois. Now all of a sudden, Oberlin is this place where all these great minds are. I was accepted and I got on campus and freaked out. I had never seen so many white people in my life. I would not get out of the car. I thought they were dirty and they stank. I thought they were contagious. I told my uncle Naw. I'm going to Howard. But my uncle coerced me into it. I freaked out for like six weeks. Classes seemed too incredibly hard. I called Dr. Salsman and cussed him out. I said, You set me up. You got me up here with all these people that's smarter than me.

The black people there were weak. Just like in high school. I was up every night workin on black people. Took over *Nommo*. Preaching at every Abusua meeting. I was a vegetarian. I was into Egyptology and Kemet and all that afrocentric encounter-stage stuff.

Encounter stage, that's when you first become aware of white racism, right? And figure out you can counteract it. How do you look back on that now?
The encounter stage is good because it takes people from hating themselves to showing them reasons why they should learn to like them-

selves. But it's lopsided. It's only half the story and it doesn't encourage people to be independent or self-reflective 'cause it's so cushiony. It's stifling. I went through it three times.

I got into all this trouble for *Nommo* from these other student groups that said it was reverse racism. Abusua said they wouldn't fund it. I said Y'all gonna be slaves forever and I went back into my shell and I've been in my shell ever since.

How'd you like Oberlin?
I thought Oberlin was magnificent. I never wanted to come home. The library was slammin. It was the first time I had the resources to match my curiosity. Access to dope professors. I only wanted to be around the smartest people and people that had traveled and been to places like London and Cairo. Intellectually, I shot off the Earth. I got scared by it though. The more As and Bs I got, the more depressed I became. People started to do the same old envy admiration bullshit as in high school. I thought I would meet people who weren't afraid of me. That sounds arrogant as hell but I don't know any other way to explain it. It keeps me lonely.

My last semester, I was like Fuck people. All I wanted was the academics. I met another drug dealer in Detroit. He was tired of the way his life was and I was tired of mine. We said, Let's get married.

Why? Why did you want to marry him?
It was someone who wasn't afraid of me. I got a perm and all my Gucci shit back. I was really the person who I was in high school. I was commuting back and forth every weekend. He bought me a car.

I was driving out of the driveway of his house to go to a job interview. It was 8 in the morning. Narcos raided both the houses on either side from where we lived. They had battering rams. Coming out of trees. Just like on TV. He's in the house 'sleep with his two sons. Both of them are named after him. *Two* Johnny Juniors. Can you imagine? And I'm supposed to be the stepmother.

So I'm pulling out of the driveway and twenty years fly past. If they come in our house that was it. I stop at a pay phone, call my mother and tell her to call him and tell him there are police on both sides of the house taking people to jail. I come back from the job interview and everything's cool. He asks how did your job interview go? That's when I start realizing how I am a tool, an instrument to raise his kids and help him launder his money—'cause I'll be a schoolteacher. I try to talk to him about it. He doesn't see a need to talk. I'm like Wait a minute. Not only have you decided what my role is, you're not even interested in hearing me protest it. So I said, Where do you want me to put this ring and car keys?

I go back to Oberlin. Graduate. My jobs starts. I think I was some kind of administrative assistant. It was a government job. They're paying us to do absolutely nothing. That was Tuesday. Wednesday, I'm back in the Detroit party scene. I'm sitting in this car watching all these people coming out of the party. Then a little voice says, You have to leave this place. You have to go to New York. My friend says, You don't know nobody in New York. Something just said go to New York. I knew a few people there from Oberlin. On Friday, I was in New York.

The first month, I stayed with Robin from Oberlin. Then I went through six months of homelessness. I'd go to the park. Meet someone. Stay at their house a couple of days. I stole food. I did the whole vagabond shit. Tryna get to Kinkos to print resumes and shit. Convinced a landlord not to make me pay a security deposit. Now I got a job and an apartment and it's time to figure out how to get into hip-hop.

My friend Chris from Oberlin was like you and hip-hop? You're the person who hated hip-hop. It was just like cartoons to me and I never really liked cartoons. I was more into other shit. Fiction. Non-fiction. Poetry. Business. My plan was to develop a portfolio writing about hip-hop then get someone to publish my first book.

So how did you become a groupie?

The first star I met was Q-Tip. I bumped into him on the street last January even before I became a writer. I saw him on Broadway and I followed him for a couple hours and eventually bumped into him at Chemical Bank. He turned around from the money machine.

Are you following me?

We were standing close enough where we coulda kissed.

I said, Yeah, somethin like dat.

He said, *dat*? Where you from?

I said, Detroit.

The lady behind me said, Are you gonna use the machine or what? We took one of those receipts and exchanged numbers. He was so fascinated that I had followed him. It was just like the video for Electric Relaxation 'cept it happened a year before. We saw each other regularly for a month then shit started to fade. He got into his music more and we started realizing we didn't like each other too much . . .

My roomate said You don't really like Jonathan, do you? You just like Q-Tip . . .

That's when I first realized I had mad groupie potential. All I had to do was revert back to my Gucci days in high school, except now I was wearing platforms.

So tell me about your life as a groupie.
Are you trying to ask me who did I have sex with?

No. That isn't nobody's business. Just, you know, other stuff.
I went to one industry party, saw all these rappers and that was it. I said, this shit is easy as hell. I could do this with my eyes closed.

KWAME AMOAKU

Do what?
Be down. That was easy. The hardest thing was getting assignments as a writer. I didn't understand the politics involved. I didn't know about query letters. And I didn't know that you don't tell everyone what your idea is because they won't assign it to you. they'll write it themselves. The more writing assignments I got, the more I saw that these other writers were doing the exact same thing I had stumbled on which was paying your rent by hanging out with stars. People say you'll play yourself as a writer.

But I had already played myself to me 'cause I participated in the exact thing that I never had respect for. Hype. All that who's-who . . . Hoopla. I was being something that I wasn't, and I took that and I pimped it.

I went ahead and did the same thing I hated people to do to me. Empty reverence. I was after fame by association. The same thing dream does in a lot of her articles. I know such-and-such, so now I'm somebody. It got to the point where I couldn't face the people I originally respected. They weren't impressed by all the things the industry people were impressed by.

Drugs. That's how I figured out I was in trouble. Because in order to stand these parties I had to be on some type of hard drugs—

and I had to buy mah drugs from de white man. It was the sickness of these parties because if you not at em it means you fallin off. People were scurrying around for ins to these parties. Who do I know at Tommy Boy? Who do I know at EMI? I was sneaking into half of these parties when I wasn't on the list. At Russell Simmons' Christmas party I slipped in with the staff wearing all-black and I hid in the bathroom for three hours until the party started. I got props for that.

How did people in New York look at you?
They thought I was dangerous. Some thought I was into voodoo. Some thought I was a straight-up drunk. I would always almost get into fights. Some thought I was a hoe, but everybody was fucking everybody. Really, you know what I was like . . .

I was like KRS-ONE. I was hip-hop and they knew it. I'm serious though. I mean think about the average hip-hop artist. Most of them ain't from the hood. I am from the hood. I had that je ne sais quoi that they were trying to capture on wax or in print (i.e. flavor). Some people thought I was crazy. I mean straight-up crazy. Some would try to hide behind their bodyguards. Some would come spend the night over my house.

Female writers would say be careful because they want to chalk us up as groupies with pens. Meanwhile everybody—you know what I'm sayin—with any type of pen . . . with the exception of Kierna Mayo . . . But the rest of them, all you have to do is figure out who you wanted to fuck. Used that journalistic license.

(This whole section was spoken with hysterical laughter)

What about the fellas?
Rap is black man's manhood now. So the black male writers use it to validate some kind of insecurity about their manhood.

Yeah. Us too.
Especially when you do one of those articles where you spend the day with them and you write an article about just chillin with the homies 'cause these little knucklehead rap artists let you hang out for the day. From the *Source* to *Vibe* to the *Village Voice* I never seen them not add some points to their little manhood rack. From the time I got there to the time I left, I watched the change in attitude. And it wasn't because of the quality of the writing. It was 'cause every time they see Big Daddy Kane or Puffy they get a pound. That's because the shit

is fake. Do you see Toni Morrison hanging around in Sweden with the people that give her the Nobel Prize?

People in New York are so microwave. I'm suspicious of things people say they did that require a lot of time or thought. I know this writer who got an assignment at a magazine and started inventing specifics based on generalities she had overheard. Instead of taking the time and doing the work or being honest and saying I bit off more than I can chew with this thing and I can't do it, she did the New York way of fakin moves and got caught. The assignment got squashed and nothing happened to her.

There are no rules in hip-hop journalism. Rap artists call the *Source* or *Vibe* when there's something they don't like. Rappers don't have any respect for hip-hop journalism because hip-hop journalists have no respect for hip-hop journalism. They just pimpin that shit and the rappers know it. That's why rappers hate press day because they know anybody who's writing about hip-hop is just a fuckin leach. They already being sucked to death by the fuckin industry. The only ones that like it are the new artists. They need the publicity. I think I lost a lot of my voice as a writer from writing about hip-hop. I appropriated this whole plastic voice.

DEEP

Is it possible to do hip-hop journalism with integrity?
Do like Nelson George. Study the art itself and the history. The only thing I respect is research. Intellectually, rappers are lazy. The smartest ones are the Five Percenters or on some kind of afrocentric tip. The Third Eye is in the middle. They can't get past the word cerebellum in the dictionary. They kick Coltrane and Dizzy in they songs as if that means something. We gotta get past that.

What about De La Soul?
De La Soul and the like have become more clever. There are a few of them that are smart. But any self-reflective growth they've achieved they've kept to themselves on account of the hip-hop literati, for fear of being exploited by these little pimps with pens. Why do you think hip-hop journalists don't get no awards? It's 'cause their shit ain't real. After awhile I just asked a lot of rappers flat-out. Leaders of the New School, MC Lyte, KRS-ONE, Black Sheep . . . They keep a lot to themselves.

So finally you just got sick of it and went back to Detroit.
I didn't have all this insight until I got out of New York and wiped all that stardust out of my eyes. A voice was saying it's time to go. No one believed I was leaving.

What's it like to be back in Detroit?
Detroit has a gray haze on top of the shit. Everybody has a gun. My little sister is getting a legal gun next year and she can't wait. Hip-hop is not high on people's list of priorities.

What about old friends?
They're all dead. Except two of them. Everybody else is dead. Yup. I hung out with guys. That's not just my story. Yup. We had metal detectors in high school long before they had them in Brooklyn. We're one of the pioneers of that whole bullshit. That's why they're not impressed by this whole gangsta rap bullshit. When Eazy E got on stage they shot at him. I heard Boss got on stage talkin bout how bad she was so they booed and threw bottles at her. Niggas was like wait wait wait. Hold on. That's why they'd rather hear about titties and ass than guns. They like Sir-Mix-A-Lot and Luke.

So where are you at now?
I'm just figuring this shit out. A month ago I felt lost and out of place. Away from anything that mattered. I wasn't empowering myself or other people. I was just coasting.

LETTERS TO VICTOR

I hate to say it but being on probation does wonders for people. That's a lot of how I got my start in journalism. Since I couldn't bomb, I started riding the train lines, taping up one page broadsheets called *It's Yours*. One of my fellow graffiti writers, Victor, had done an illustration for *It's Yours* in 1989 and not all that much constructive since. Last fall, he called me to say he was on probation. And guess what? He was starting a paper.

Dear Victor,

Well it's about time you start a paper! Journalism is really failing. The supply of and demand for intelligent, pertinent journalism is thin and thinning. It's thinnest of all among kids our age, the I-don't-have-patience-for-anything generation.

Who can blame us? Daily papers are boring and irrelevant. The really clever and interesting writing is way over our heads. All we are left with, the only printed matter that is both in-

ANTCK

triguing to us and intellectually available, is the popular horror, self-help, comedy, romance, and celebrity bios are just as dumb as we are. Any direction we turn, we are surrounded by swamps of stupidity.

Rap is in many ways our attempt as a generation to fill in the literary gap left by the abandonment of good books. Rap is a glimmer of hope, but let's face it, most rap is dumb too. The job of the hip-hop journalist is to capture the attentions of the rap listeners and to sharpen their thinking at the same time.

Most hip-hop journalism fails on both counts. It isn't sharp or skeptical enough to be journalism and it isn't alive enough to be hip-hop (when was the last time you heard of a rapper quoting a magazine instead of the other way around?). It is too mesmerized by fame and personality and the music industry, and it is too stale and too dumb and too long-winded (when was the last time you read a hip-hop magazine cover to cover?). And it doesn't reach most of its potential audience.

Thems that write about hip-hop aren't close enough to it, and thems that are close to hip-hop don't know how to write, let alone edit, sell ads, organize a staff and publish a paper—which gets you even further away from hip-hop and the inner-city you are supposed to be serving. The people you most want to reach are the people you are least likely to reach. So not only do you have to supply good journalism, you also have to create the demand for it. I think you should name the paper "Fuck the Suburbs" or "Fuck Hip-hop." Something that will grab the attention of people who wouldn't otherwise read. And writing it real big and posting it up all over the city.

Dec. 1993

Dear Victor,

I guess you're right. It would be kind of hard to finance a paper called *Fuck the Suburbs*. Maybe next time.

If I understand the idea you guys settled on, it sounds like a good compromise. You're going to publish a two sided broadsheet called *Subway and Elevated*. The Subway side, you'll pull everyone's card who the other papers won't touch. The Elevated side, you will tackle things that are too . . . elevated for other papers—like actual strategies and solutions.

Subway and Elevated. Yup, those are the gaps alright. And the two sides will contradict each other so that you can get at the multifaceted nature of truth.

You want to reach people who wouldn't otherwise read. Okay. You're going to keep the format short and surprising so readers can read the whole thing. Okay. Instead of big-ass ads, you'll have cute little sponsors. Okay. And you're going to post it up on the train lines. Yeah, I like that. It doesn't sound like you'll be making any money at this. Just be careful to set things up for yourself so you don't burn out.

Let me tell you about burning out. Back in the good ol days of 1988, there were only about six hip-hop publications nationwide. There was *IGT* in New York. There was *GSXL* in Queens. There was *Ghetto Art* in California. There was *On the Go* in Philadelphia. There was *The Source* in Boston. And there was *It's Yours* in Chicago, the only publication in the history of hip-hop to be posted up on train lines, the only one that treated hip-hop not as a members-only club but as a television screen for the inner-city. I was so proud of *It's Yours*. By comparison, all the other papers were isolationist and narrow.

But look where the other publications are today. *IGT* has maintained itself for its heavily international (Australian, European) audience as the liveliest, and most authentic document of New York City graffiti. *GSXL* became *Beatdown*. *Ghetto Art* turned into *Can Control*, the biggest circulation graffiti magazine in the world. *On the Go* became the buck-wild, hilarious magazine that makes all the other magazines look retarded. *The Source* became *The Source*. And *It's Yours* from Chicago got burnt out.

In a way, this has been the story of everything interesting that has come out of Chicago hip-hop. Too many of us had too much integrity and too little business sense. Hell, why do so many of us still breakdance? Why do so many of us still beatbox? The two most successful rappers to come out of Chicago, Common Sense and The Brat, had nothing to do with the city-wide hip-hop scene.

Although we have come to love Common Sense for his lyrical brilliance, there are a lot of us here who feel frus-trated. Nobody listens to knowledge rap-pers anymore, Common Sense seemed to be saying on his first album: Some step with concepts, but um, who cares? Not even the damn people under the stairs.

So welcome to the club. If you want to make a paper in the legacy of *It's Yours*, you have to realize that even if you succeed, it will never put you in a category of even the lowliest employee of *The Source*. You will not get free CDs and promotional items in the mail. You will not be able to use it on a resume and you will not be on your way to a salaried job in publishing, adver-tising, or the music industry. You will have to find your re-wards elsewhere. Your life will be more like that of a com-munity organizer, a school teacher, or just a permanently unsigned rapper. You'll probably get a lot of letters like this:

69

Yo Editor,

Yo kid! I'm writin' this letter to drop some science on you about your wack new paper, kid! Yo kid! What's up with one page? That ain't no real hip-hop paper, you know what I'm sayin? That ain't flavor. That ain't phat. So sit back, relax, and let me drop some science on you kid.

First of all, to be a hip-hop magazine, you need to get interviews of famous rappers. After that, you can add other features into the paper like: columns, ads, record reviews, ads, demo reviews, ads, Graph Flicks, ads, phashion, ads, news pertaining to the music industry with regards to the Chicago hip-hop market, and a whole lot of ads.

And yo kid, when you get really large like I am which will never be, you can add in sections that are all about you: a Letter from the Editor, a Letter from the Publisher, a Letter from the Editor to the Publisher, a page for letters and articles about the Editor and the Publisher, a table of contents page, and a page where you take flix of people chillin' on the scene and give your shout-outs to all the fly hardcore TRUE hip-hoppers . . . like me.

Yo kid, who are you anyway? What's up with not signing names on the articles tip, kid? Yo kid, you need to come correct on the represent tip, kid. One side of your paper you say one thing. Then the other side you say somethin' else. That's straight-up contradict on the intellect tip kid! Yo kid, I feel sorry for you. You ain't dope kid. Yo kid, you don't know shit about hip-hop. You ain't undaground kid. Yo kid, I have spoken.

Publisher Gusto
CB4 Magazine

Then you may have your own letters to write. Here is an abridged version of a letter I sent to *Dry-Paper* a couple of months ago. We have ironed out a lot of our personal differences since then, and all things considered, *Dry-Paper* is in a lot of ways a really good paper. But we still disagree about a lot of things, one of which is that a paper has the responsibility to print letters that criticize it. *Dry-Paper* has politely refused to print [the original of] this letter. They said it was too long.

Dear *Dry-Paper* :

In the Fall 1993 issue, Ronald O'Neal implied that he appreciated constructive criticism (O'Neal 38). Here are some of mine:

1. Please don't write (38) that I submitted "We Use Words Like Mackadocious" to anyone at Dry-Paper. (If so, where's your copy of it?) The Source assigned me to write that story exclusively for them in April 1992 (before *Dry-Paper* existed in any form).

2. Please do not say or imply that you or anyone else is "hip-hop" unless you or they are proficient in at least one of the following: (1) MCing (2) Beat making (3) Graffiti (4) B-boying or flexing. And can back it up in a battle.

3. Please do not say or imply that *Dry-Paper* is "undaground hip-hop" until more than half of its content, page for page, focuses on subjects which are unknown, not commercially available, or otherwise deserving of the term "underground" *and* more than half of the contributions, page for page, are made by people fitting the descriptions "underground" and "hip-hop"—as defined above, or by any other useful definitions of these terms.

4. Please do not say or imply that *Dry-Paper* is "strictly" undaground hip-hop until *all* of its content fits that description.

5. If you have something to say, say it. Please do not run anonymous news articles in which you quote yourself, as you did on page 24 of the Fall '93 issue.

6. When you call up my editor at The Source to complain about an article I wrote, and then let him describe you as "citing rhymers Common Sense, DA Smart, Kinetic Order, Children of Reality, and Bla Zae Blah [SIC] along with events at the China Club, as evidence of the upswing in hip-hop momentum (May '93)" please inform him that you are speaking *not only as a journalist*, but as the *manager* of Kinetic Order and Children of Reality, and as the *promoter* of those very events at the China Club, and that it is a conflict of interest for you to promote your own business projects as a journalist.

7) Please do not represent *Dry-Paper* as journalism or

yourself as a journalist (O'Neal 27) until you explicitly *label as advertisement* all articles that promote you and New Jack Enterprises' other business ventures. Yes, this goes on at other trade publications and it is a disgrace there also. Many professional journalists would be fired for half of the conflicts of interest you have taken part in. It is a violation of the public trust and an insult to the whole idea of journalism. Also, although it is less clear-cut than business conflicts, please be sure not to call yourself a journalist until your personal friendships and allegiances stop showing up as *Dry-Paper* coverage.

8. Please do not represent yourself as a spokesperson for Chicago hip-hop in such media outlets as: The Source, WBEZ, Rappages, Billboard, Crain's Chicago Business, The Chicago Tribune, and The Chicago Sun-Times until you have earned the respect of those pillars of Chicago's hip-hop community who:

A. Stuck with hip-hop through (what Kirk from the West Side calls) "the hip-hop drought" from 1987-'90.

B. Aren't so polite, business-minded, uninterested, or desperately eager to please that they won't pull your card when you fuck-up editorially. (If you had solicited advice from these people in the first place, I would not be sitting here right now, pointing out to you all of these basic tenets of hip-hop, journalism, and common decency.)

9. Please do not represent yourself as a spokesperson for the entire Midwest (O'Neal 38) until you have done the same for Milwaukee, St. Louis, Detroit, Indianapolis, Cleveland, and any other cities with significant hip-hop scenes. (Representing yourself as a spokesperson for "Young black business leaders" is not something for me to pass judgment on.)

10. If you feel you cannot resist the temptation (inside and outside *Dry-Paper* itself) to use your journalistic credibility as a vehicle for advancing your own narrow personal and business interests, then you should consider selling *Dry-Paper* and turning over its editorial content to people for whom it would not create such a conflict of interest (such as your own staffers Scoop Jackson and B-Boy B). You would then be free to go off and become a manager/superpromot-

er—both of which you seem to be incredibly good at—while leaving the hip-hop journalism to a hip-hopper and a journalist.

11. Please disregard any criticisms of you I have made that I myself have failed to deliver on. (And please point them out to me if you think there are any!) Covering and nurturing Chicago hip-hop has been a serious job to me and so far, Ronald, you've been my most outspoken critic. I appreciate your fearlessness and I hope I can depend on you for criticism in the future.

12. As for the criticism you have already given (that my article "We Use Words Like Mackadocious" was "ridiculous," "garbage," and "a mistake") I was hoping for something a little more specific. After the other one hundred or so letters that people sent critiquing my article, I was particularly interested to know your reaction, because the rest of the critics—except two of Hubby's other rap industry friends—were all white kids.

The few people who responded favorably to the article were mostly black and Latino readers. Sheena Lester of *Rappages*, for example, called it the "best article [in six months]." Yet, like so many of the white kids who wrote in, you dismissed it as "garbage." If, as you say, you want your beliefs and actions to be "duplicatable" and "accessible" to black youth (O'Neal 27), would you care to give a duplicatable, accessible explanation of your views, other than the fact that Huffy is your friend and I'm not?

Of course Horsey's response was "intelligent".* Most

---

* *The Source*, July 1993—"Contrary to what Upski may think or hope, I am not responding to 'We Use Words Like Mackadocious' to defend my 'downness' or even attempt to fuck him up the way he did me. I am also not going to defend or dis all white people who listen to hip-hop because I am not in a position to do so. I can only refer to what I know and feel about hip-hop. I do not listen to and write about hip-hop for props, social acceptance from non-whites, or to attempt to exempt and redeem myself from the actions of Europeans throughout history. I can only speak for me, Hokie Shoeswinger, whose full name and pen name (without permission, may I add) was dragged through some serious-ass bullshit. The intention of my inclusion in the article is obviously the result of some kind of personal beef Upski has with myself. My portrayal in the article was that of mad ignorance and insecurity. As another writer of hip-hop, I am fully open to skeptical minds and questions concerning my feelings toward hip-hop and my place in it. I am a politically conscious hip-hop listener who celebrates its spirit, not someone trying to be black or belittle the origins of hip-hop as an expression of struggling black youth. Upski played me like the Lady Di of hip-hop in this magazine that is read like the Bible of hip-hop. He did exactly what he dissed in the article: trying to prove and legitimize his own intentions by judging and publishing mine."

people who went to New Trier High School can write intelligent responses. She intelligently avoided the whole point of her inclusion in the article: the phenomenon of a suburban white who got interested in hip-hop, and within one year had a newspaper column writing about it (and now a job in the industry!).

I mean what a sucker I was to spend those five years, more than 100 pieces, eight arrests, and 40,000 copies of profitless homemade publications distributed on bus and train lines before I started writing for a then-obscure maga-

RAVEN

zine called *The Source* . And to think that I actually felt lucky because I knew I hardly paid any dues compared to a lot of people who weren't nearly as successful. What a fool I was! I could have just come on the scene in 1992, gotten everything right away, and explained myself intelligently to the satisfaction of my black editor.

Amazingly Harply, you responded to my article without ever addressing any of my actual points. The accusations you are responding to are not accusations that I made. Go back and read the article. I never judged your intentions or motivations for being involved in hip-hop. I never judged whether you are ignorant and insecure or not, I never judged your "feelings toward hip-hop" or how you see yourself with respect to the history of race relations. I also never said whether I felt you were open-minded or not, and I certainly never said you were "trying to be black" (whatever that means). All of that is your personal business, and all of it is beside the point.

What I focused on were questions such as: How does a white person from the suburbs suddenly obtain a newspaper column articulating the issues and sensibilities of Chicago hip-hop within a year of arriving on the scene? How does such a person rise to such a position at a fraction of the dues?

You write that you celebrate the spirit of hip-hop, but the spirit of hip-hop has been around for decades. Where were you even as recently as three years ago? (You too, Ronald and Mic.)

What mindset allows you to justify to yourself the job you now have in the industry when hip-hoppers who have paid tons more dues than you can hardly find work at all? What, if anything, can be done about people like you and me—and whose responsibility would it be? These are the questions I was asking. You write that you are "politically conscious" and "fully open to skeptical minds and questions." Where is your "politically conscious" and "fully open" *reply to the issues* I was raising by including you in my article?

If you want to disagree with me, you have to begin by responding to my points. Implying that I am a hypocrite with bad intentions was a good start. At least it would have been if I hadn't said it myself in my own article (and by the way, that is *not* what I was dissing. I believe it applies to everyone.) Otherwise, your only discussion of any issues was to say that you were in no position to have a position. Can't go wrong there, can you?

It's true that I am not in a "position" to "dis all whites in hip-hop" any more than anyone else. I was just making observations about the way you present yourself, and speculating, using my own experience, about what you were probably thinking at the time. That doesn't make me higher than anybody. It just means that it's white people's job to keep each other in check instead of always making black people have to deal with us. But your purpose in the story was only as an illustration of a bigger point. If you feel your shoes ain't untied then don't even trip.

As for your objection to being fully named and identified,

it's kind of babyish, don't you think? What do you have to hide? I don't have anything to hide professionally. No responsible journalist should. You can come to my house and look through all my closets.

13. Ronald, I think a lot of the points I have raised here are serious, not only for me but for hip-hop as a whole in Chicago. If you agree, please print those parts of my letter in *Dry-Paper* and respond to them publicly. And please allow readers, including me, space for a rebuttal.

14. I hope you don't think I'm singling out *The Source*. I've written critically about other publications, including *The Source* and the *Chicago Tribune*. For example, I once wrote a letter to Chris Wilder and James Bernard, the highest-ranking black editors at *The Source*, asking them if there was anything I could do to help convince the white executives, Jon Shecter and David Mays, to resign—as a matter of principle—and let *The Source* be fully black-owned.

I didn't write that because I dislike Jon Shecter and David Mays. David Mays signs my checks! Jon Shecter is cool with me too, and although I disagree with him about a lot of things, I think that for the most part he's a really good editor. I also like Geoffrey Watts who used to write *The Source*'s Chicago Report, and I like Artistic who edits the Chi-Rock magazine, and I like the rap group Stony Island, but as all of them can tell you, I let them know loud and clear when I think they fuck up and I expect them to do the same for me. So it's not like you're being singled out.

Sincerely, sincerely, etc. etc.

Jan. 1994

Dear Victor,

You've been working on *Subway and Elevated* for a couple of months now, but it seems you have skipped an important step. To publish a magazine you have to read. You have to read books. You have to read books because books are where some of the cleverest people in history have recorded their thoughts. But that's only a few books. Most books—including, I suspect, most of the books you read—suck. They are a waste of time. As Mark Twain said, the man who does not read good books has no advantage over

the man who can't read.

That's why there are magazines. Magazines are a waste of time too, but they are a waste of less time than books. Start by browsing through a library and reading whatever is fun for you. You should read as a challenge, never as a chore. The goal of reading is less to gain knowledge than to sharpen your wits. Read not for the facts but for the angles of thinking. Read writers who are sharper than you and sharpen your mind against theirs. The sharper your mind becomes, the better the magazines you will read. The goal is to sharpen your mind to a point where the only magazines that don't bore you are the freshest magazines in the country. Then you narrow it down to the freshest writers in the freshest magazines. Then you find out their favorite books.

For the serious writer, Hemingway goes even farther: "There is no use writing anything that has been written before unless you can beat it . . . Most live writers do not exist. Their fame is created by critics who always need a genius of the season, someone they understand completely and feel safe in praising, but when these fabricated geniuses are dead they will not exist. The only people for a serious writer to compete with are the dead that he knows are good. It is like the miler running against the clock rather than simply trying to beat whoever is in the race with him. Unless he runs against time, he will never know what he is capable of attaining."

But that's down the road. You can start by getting familiar with: *Emerge, The Village Voice, Mother Jones, Utne Reader, Rolling Stone, National Review, Esquire* (where the Hemingway quote first appeared), *Ms., The Source, Vibe, Spin, Rappages* and other pushy, sexy magazines. Not all the articles in these magazines are good. But they usually run at least one strong article in each issue.

When reading about hip-hop, pay special attention to writers like Nelson George (the godfather of hip-hop journalism)*, James Bernard, Rob Marriot, Scott Poulson-Bryant, Reginald Dennis, Sheena Lester, Greg Tate (when you can make it through his wordology), Bonz Malone (when you can make it through his wordology), Danyel Smith, Scoop Jackson, Da Ghetto Communicator, Cheo Coker, Adario Strange, Ronin Ro, The Rap Bandit, dream hampton, Harry Allen, Mark Surface, Bobbito, and others who you'll soon be telling me about. But again, don't let hip-hop take up more than 10 to 15% of your literary diet.

These are some of the magazines you should be reaching for: *The Atlantic Monthly, Harper's, The New Republic, The New Yorker,* and *The Nation.* You won't like these magazines immediately. They're not always very likable. Start by eavesdropping on the debates in the letters pages. Little by little, you'll familiarize yourself with the territory. You'll start to get more of the jokes. The references will begin to mean something to you. You'll get to know the writers. You'll make it a point to stop in periodical stands daily to read articles. Before you know it, you'll have passed into the same league intellectually as college professors, Bill Clinton, and the Executive Editor of *The New York Times.* You are now in a position to play ball with them and to take advantage of all that the modern world has to offer—including, if

---

* Or as Lesley Thomas says: He's not the godfather of hip-hop journalism. He's just the only one.

you so choose, to publish a world-class broadsheet on the Chicago transit system.

Mar. 1994

Dear Victor,

Hooray! *Subway and Elevated* is great! Riding the train today, I saw a series of them taped against the pillars in Jackson station. I jumped off the train, tore one down (sorry about that), and read the whole thing right there on the spot. Then I read it aloud to the commuters who were waiting for the train.

Will you publish my first book?

May 1994

Dear Victor,

I warned you about this earlier, and I see it becoming more and more of a problem. The whitening of *Subway and Elevated*. I remember coming to meetings last fall and being the only white face. Now you're expanding your operation and getting response mail. You need money and more dependable, experienced writers. More and more you will begin to feel like the people who most appreciate you, and who can help you the most are not only white, but further and further away from the audience you were originally seeking to target. And that is an audience that doesn't usually buy ads or write letters to the editor.

You have bumped up against the exact reason why nobody does a good job of reaching that audience. That is also the exact reason they have become so isolated and cut off from the rest of society, which is exactly the reason we have these problems in the first place. Resist the temptation to let *Subway and Elevated* be whitenized Victor. There are thousands of magazines out there for middle-class graffiti artists, coffee-sippers, college students, rap fans, and leftists. There is nothing intelligent written for inner-city grammar school, high-school, and junior college kids, drop-outs, criminals, teenage mothers, gangbangers, and would-be hip-hoppers. For people who memorize rap lyrics but don't feel reading is for them. That's where you came from Victor, and if the paper has any integrity, that's the direction it needs to go in.

FAKING THE CONVERSATION

"What is the funk and how will I know if I'm faking it?"

—DEL THE FUNKY HOMOSAPIEN (1991)

Two years later, people are still talking about "faking the funk" as though it meant something, as though Del had never even posed the question.

Funk is an aesthetic, a sensibility.

Funk is not something that is possible to fake. It can be mocked or misrepresented. It can be harnessed to create products which are bought and sold. It can be attacked and ridiculed—aren't *these* what we really mean when we say "*faking* the funk"?

Haven't we just been using the wrong verb?

And if so (here comes the bigger question), what do we really mean by the whole REAL vs. FAKE campaign in hip-hop? Crazy Legs wearing a "True Skool" T-shirt . . . KRS-ONE asking, "How many REAL hip-hoppers in the place right about now?" Aren't these just our attempt as a community to pass moral judgment—to separate the good stuff from the junk"—without sounding corny?

There's no problem with that. No one doubts that KRS-ONE is a real hip-hopper, whatever that is, or that Crazy Legs is from the True Skool, whatever that is. The only problem: What the fuck is it?

The only problem, as Large Professor says: We've got to be more precise. It's like Moses coming down off Mount Sinai with The Two Commandments: "Stay True," and "Don't Fake": unless we can agree

ERICA THORNTON

on what they mean in an actual situation, what's the point of even bringing them up?

Some will say that phrases like "fake" and "real" are intentionally vague and undefinable, that "We know what we mean" when we use them and defining them will stifle hip-hop by placing restrictions on it.

Okay . . .Alice Walker, about this book title . . .it's so exact, are you sure you want to *limit* yourself to purple? You could be *stifling* your subject matter. Why not just call it "The Real Color"—real readers will know what you mean . . . Oh, Mr. Shakespeare, *Romeo and Juliet*? But this is a *universal* story. You don't want people to think it was limited to one couple! Let's call it "Real Love" . . . Mr. Haley, Mr. Haley, *Mister Haley*! Why are you trying to label this as an *autobiography*? It's so much more than just a life story! "The Real Malcolm X"—that's what you should call it . . .

The creative side of hip-hop should never be stifled. Using more precise language doesn't stifle. It lets us say what we mean. If hip-hop is going to have a moral side, it must be specific enough to be useful. Otherwise, every time we say something like "Be true to the game," what the fuck are we even talking about?

And how can we begin to protect "real hip-hop" from exploitation if we can't say exactly what it is that we are protecting? If we can't answer Del's question about how to tell the difference between real and fake, who are we to say that we ourselves aren't fake?

That's why authenticity is such a dead-end street. If we're gonna talk morals, let's keep the discussion in this atmosphere: Word is bond; pay your dues; don't front; don't bite; don't stop; don't forget where you came from; peace, unity, love and having fun; give credit where it's due; show and prove; stop the violence; freedom of speech; don't wish on a four-leaf clover; do for self; it ain't where you're from it where ya at; and give back to whoever made you what you are . . . (And it ain't always easy. Contradictory morals, such as "It ain't where ya from, it's where ya at," and "Don't forget where you came from" need some sorting out.)

But most morals just need to be brought down to Earth with specifics: What exactly are my dues? *How* must I pay them, *in what form* and *to whom*? *When* do I have to start paying them, and when do I get to stop and have other people pay dues to me? *How* are my dues different from someone else's of a different race or class? From a different city? At a different time? In a different hip-hop art form or in more than one art form? *Why* do I have to pay dues in the first place, and *who's* to say whether I'm in debt?

Until we begin posing and answering our moral questions at a more practical, precise, and specific level, what we're really mocking, misrepresenting, buying, selling, stifling, attacking, ridiculing, and yes, faking, is the whole conversation of what we believe in and how we want to live. **(1993)**

THE CHICAGO SYNDROME

"But if Harlem is our spiritual home, Chicago, particularly its South Side, is our dark, chocolate soul."

—NELSON GEORGE, 1991

Even before the sun has gone down on 53rd Street, Salahdin is on the block. Back and forth he walks, between the viaduct and the park, wearing semi-respectable clothes, his lower lip trembling because he has a plastic bag of crack in his cheek. If the police come, Salahdin will swallow the bag. If the customer is a plain-clothes cop, he will go to jail. If the crack business is slow though, you can convince Salahdin to come chill in the park for a while and kick his latest rhyme for you—even though he's got other things on his mind.

Salahdin memorizes all his rhymes; he has no home, nowhere to write them down. His voice seems to come from his chest; he summons it forth slow, off-beat, compelling, it erupts from his throat as from the throat of a volcano, he brings it down on you like the last punches of a fight, every blow falling in stupefying slow-motion. "You feel I'm not fair / But still war was declared / Will you be rollin? / Yeah, in a wheelchair."

Salahdin himself now rolls in a wheelchair. Drunk one night while trying to enter an apartment by kicking in the air conditioner (similar to the way he entered my apartment in a desperate moment a few years back), Salahdin slipped off a fire escape "somehow," and survived the eleven story fall by grabbing shit on the way down. In his hospital bed, he reads Poe, and fills a notebook with new lyrics.

Salahdin notices you are carrying a rap magazine which you just picked up from the store. (Actually, you stole it from the store. It had your article in it and the fuckers never sent you a copy.) Salahdin wants to read it. He studies the pages for half an hour, sitting on a park bench with you looking over his shoulder. You laugh about some stupid shit together. You want to hear more rhymes; Salahdin must return to work.

Salahdin's 53rd Street on Chicago's South Side is part of the biggest ghetto of untapped lyrical talent on the continent (although as you read this the tapping has already begun). It is nearly ten times the size of either Harlem or Compton.

Hip-hop in Chicago got off to a slow start. In 1974, six New York graffiti writers tried to introduce graffiti to Chicago's Blackstone Rangers: "We had a great meeting with these dudes, these hoodlums!" recalled Bama UGA. "These massive seventy-five big black boys who were out to kill us. They said 'Y'all from New York. Y'all supposed to be bad.' Why we were there was because we were supposed to be setting them up with this program . . . where they make a little bit of change and do something constructive. But their idea of something constructive is selling cocaine and getting two bills a week sitting back on their asses and scaring people."*

---

* Quoted in Craig Castleman's *Getting Up*. Cambridge, Mass.: MIT Press, 1982.

But in an age when record companies can transform 13-year-old kids at a mall into major rap artists, America's third largest city isn't even as renowned as Seattle, Houston, or Miami—let alone NO PLASE (New York / Oakland / Philly / Los Angeles / Atlanta / San Francisco / England).

Chicago is a mammoth symbol for what the *other* ninety-nine percent of the hip-hop nation is really like: ordinary stiffs like Salahdin for whom rap means creativity and struggle, not fame and fortune. These are the magazine readers, the demo senders, the contest mongers, the business blockheads, the lazy, the undeserving, those who have tried, those who will try anything, everything, to be one of the few artists selected by the music industry to make it.

Every demo sent out is a sacrifice of clothing, rent, child support, bus fare or food. People here are frustrated. Even going to a concert makes some rappers miserable. "It hurts to see these kids up there on stage getting paid for a gimmick when those who've been hip-hopping all these years are still in the audience," says Ang 13.

"You've got night club owners on every street corner trying to exploit rappers," says South Side rapper Witch 1. "They'll have a $500 rap contest. They have you pay $20 to enter. You not guaranteed to get in. They charge $5 at the door. And then they have it rigged for these two dufus-ass girls who didn't nobody like to win."

Some of them try so hard to beat the odds. They print calling cards but their phone gets disconnected. The gap between Chicago's real rap talent and the industry's real talent makers became self-widening, propelled by the inability of the movers and shakers on either side to find each other.

While most of Chicago's rappers are nothing more than pathetic imitations of already popular artists, a few of the more original acts are staking out a multi-faceted, but distinctly Chicago sensibility. The sensibility grows out of Chicago's long and painful memory as the underdog of the rap industry. While famous rappers make songs about their cars, concerts, the trials of the music industry and of being a star, Chicago rappers don't tend to be experienced in those matters.

Within the last few years, slowly, Chicago has begun to recover from Chicago syndrome. A couple of groups have gotten a foot in the door with many others on their way. Chicago's rappers are now trying desperately to catch-up to their counterparts in other cities. If you ain't from NO PLASE, and you have fresh ideas—and persistence—you will probably still be appreciated someplace.

Even Salahdin might get his act together someday and get rec. But what about the Chicago syndrome in the rest of the country? How many Salahdins are there in Detroit, Cleveland, Milwaukee, St. Louis, Buffalo, Pittsburgh, Jackson, Raleigh, Norfolk, Richmond, Sacramento, Columbus, Indianapolis, Nashville, Minneapolis-St. Paul, Providence, Portland, Toronto, Toledo, Hartford (excluding The Skinny Boys), New Haven, Knoxville, Rochester, Birmingham, Boston, Montgomery, Cincinnati, Columbia, Kansas City, San Antonio, Las Vegas, Louisville, Charleston, Tampa, Tulsa, Memphis, Montreal, Denver, Baltimore, New Orleans—and everywhere in between?

As Aaron Brown says: I ain't into all that New York-LA-Chicago bullshit. That's called tribalism. That's when you too stupid to understand that other people go through the same shit as you . . . None of us came over here on the love boat!

The reality is, even if they do get signed, most will never get rich and famous off of rap. But as long as there's bread on the table, those who get the most out of hip-hop are those who do it just for its own sake. The ones who work their butts off just because it makes them feel alive. The ones for whom talking and freestyling are one and the same. The ones whose very words make the soul turn. The ones for whom every record store is a gold mine of sound, every library a heaven of language, and every street corner an open mic. The ones for whom every listener is a life, not a screaming dot in the 29th row. These are the ones who really know what hip-hop is about. They don't need to try and "make it" because they already have. **(1991)**

An Interview with Aaron Brown

HOW NOT TO BE
TAKEN ADVANTAGE OF

Aaron Brown knows how not to be taken advantage of. Of all the people I've dealt with in this book, he is the only one who asked to be paid. MCing since 1981, Aaron Brown and his group Ten Tray were the first Chicago artists to release an album on a major label. I had never thought of paying someone for an interview before, but when I thought about it, it only seemed fair. Subway and Elevated decided to pay people interviewed five precent of the royalties from the book.

That wasn't good enough for Aaron. He wanted to be paid up front. "Let me put it to you like this," he said. "Any funds that I get go to one of our programs working with youth. I'm not just accountable to myself. If it was just me, I wouldn't care. I'm part of a community that I have to be accountable to. When they say 'why did you do this interview? How does it benefit the community?' I had better have a good reason. I got paid $2,500 speaking at Columbia College. Right now, we need $250 for a camping trip to buy the kids sleeping bags or whatever. We have to come out of our pockets for a lot of this stuff. You can't talk to someone about culture if they're thinking about putting food in their stomach."

I gave him his money. And because of him, other people are getting paid too.

AARON: Since I started, rap has gone from an expression of the soul of the people to a tool of exploitation. The new rap lacks that substance. You don't hear rappers like Melle Mel anymore. When you look at R&B music between '66 and '72, it was mostly political. James Brown made "I'm Black And I'm Proud". Aretha Franklin, Curtis Mayfield, The Four Tops. The Temptations even made a lot of political songs. It wasn't until the '70s when you stopped hearing the struggle and you started hearing all the Super Fly stuff. Rap is taking that same turn.

I just realized that almost fifteen years ago I used to battle cats out in front of Kenwood. The person who got me into history and culture was Minister Farrakhan, seeing him tell Phil Donahue off on TV. It didn't stop me from doing what wasn't right but it opened a door in my consciousness. I've done a lot of things in the past. I used to sell drugs. I was drinking, smoking reefer. A lot of that came between the time I was 17 and 20 so it wasn't that long ago.

Black people don't have control over our destiny. Even though PE sold millions of albums, nothing much has changed as a result of it. The problem is, there's no institution for liberation the music can reflect. If you have no institution for your people to reinforce your music, then you're really wasting your time. All your songs make no difference. Gang Starr made conscious music but not as much anymore. It's part of a historic pattern. The Blues at one time was very political. Reggae was very political with the elder dreads. Now you see what reggae has been reduced to. Now you can't talk about four hundred years. You have to talk about poom-poom. Punani.

Take a group like Arrested Development. When they first came out they were very, very political, heavily into the culture. Then they had a crossover hit with "Everyday People" and I started seeing them wearing red, white and blue. This is not an indictment of Arrested Development. In order to reach a broader audience they were persuaded to change their image. I believe this is what happened because this was attempted with us before we split with Polygram.

We were very blunt in our music. We named Africans who had been murdered: Fred Hampton, Yusef Hawkins, Malcolm X, Martin Luther King, and we didn't hesitate to place the responsibility. We received no promotions. No press. The record company told us on the next album to do more crossover songs along the lines of Arrested Development. They even asked us if we could dress like X-Klan.

Most political songs were acceptable because they weren't a threat. It's one thing to be political. It's another thing to be political and to know what you're talking about. The hardest song PE made to me was "Black Steel in the Hour of Chaos" about brothers revolting in a prison. The Hardest song KRS-ONE made was "Why is That?". It was a wonderful song. I loved it. But it sounded like academia to me. It was about what was said in the Bible. And to brothers on the street, it wasn't about things in their everyday experience.

I've never heard a rap group—a music group for that matter—whose values were Afrikan. Walked the walk and had everything in order. The music industry is wicked. Being in the industry is like being a virgin in a whorehouse. Either you leave or you become a prostitute. I didn't go all the way in, but I went far enough in where I had meetings that made me sick to my stomach.

It's not that a lot of the artists don't have good intentions. In the '60s, there was a movement that was holding

musicians accountable. When the movement was destroyed, you started seeing music groups moving away from the struggle into what was popular or acceptable to this country or in the industry. Right now, there is no movement to hold people accountable. Artists need to align themselves with serious and powerful organizations. See, if you just

from: Publicity dept.
to: Bob Belcaster, CTA President.

re: Here's the artwork you requested for the new Green Line poster campaign,
part of our on-going effort to reach out to ethnic communities by matching
train lines with their favorite food groups. "The Orange Line," as you'll
recall, was targeted to old Polish grannies living out by Midway Airport.
(dreaming they'll retire to Florida.) For the blacks, it was between this
and "The Collard Green Line"... They both sounded pretty good to me Bob.

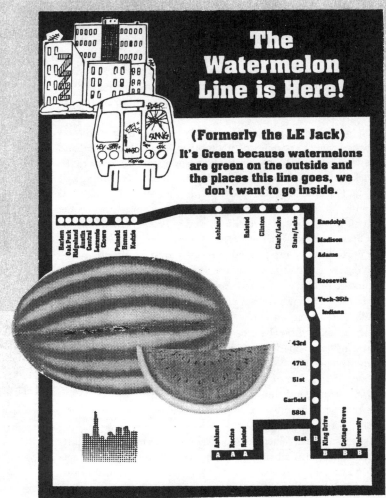

ps. Can I get a bonus for this?

read a few books about the struggle and write some rhymes representing it, you can still lose your focus and be taken advantage of because you don't have a base of values to protect yourself.

I'm part of a community, I'm under the guidance of people who've been in the struggle twenty-five to thirty years. Now unless you're retarded, your music is going to reflect that community that you're a part of. It's consistency. Like somebody that marched with King in Cicero. Now you live in Northbrook talking about what you've done for the struggle. Why do you have to sit on your laurels? You have to make up your mind whether or not you're willing to bend over. I don't want to deal with the industry. I'm tired of giving eighty-five percent of what I make to them. I never received more than $500 in my pocket from record royalties.

My opinion is that black people are not free. We are in a worse condition now than in 1850. Look at our communities. The police department is an occupying force. They're involved in the drug trade. So are Arab businesses. Our communities are under attack. The next step is having seven o'clock curfews and putting every young black man who's been in trouble into boot camps.

Look what they did to the Jews in Germany. First they put them in ghettos. No first they destabilized the economy. Then ghettos. Then concentration camps. Then extermination camps.

We're rebuilding the Afrikan personality which has been destroyed as a result of the worst crime in history called the Afrikan slave trade by Europeans. In Afrika, it was called the Disaster. That's what I call it. It wasn't a trade to us. We didn't trade anything. Europeans created all these problems.

Look at today. You crush the family structure in the community. You create all the economic conditions for people to sell drugs on the corner. Then you offer solutions to put them into boot camps. And we agree with you because we feel we can't control our own problems. This is not racist, it's reality. You have to look at the source of a problem, not the symptoms as Europeans teach us.

It's not white people's right or responsibility to say "What can we do to help you in the black community?" If European-Americans are serious about atonement and changing, they need to study the real world history, and the real numbers of the real Holocaust. No one even said they were sorry—not that that would be repayment. If white people are going to organize, they need to organize amongst themselves around these injustices.

We've been put in the position of coping, survival. To cope, you have to learn how to be submissive, be cool. Carter G. Woodson, the man who invented Black History Month said "If you control a man's thoughts, you don't have to worry about his actions." We're thinking the thoughts of the oppressor. We're taught to hate Afrika. We're taught that it's savage, when in fact history proves civilization began in Afrika. We had the first math, the first science, doctors, black-smiths, the first people that taught languages were in Afrika.

This information can be found in books such as: *The Destruction of Black Civilization* by Chancellor Williams; *2000 Seasons* by Ayi Kwei Armah; *Africa's Gift to America* by J.A. Rogers; and *What They Never Taught You in History Class* by Indus Khamit-Kush.

These books are nothing but good reading, inspirational. The key is not to have a race full of intellectuals with degrees in the European educational system. It's about making Afrikan culture live through your actions. I know a lot of people who can say the same things I've said, go on a college speaking circuit, get $5,000 a talk and live fat while Afrikan babies are starving. I'm a self-educated man. Yeah, I went to Kenwood which was an integrated school. Yeah I went to a white college and I had a black intellectual there who taught me, but it didn't keep me from going into a negative role. The elders I look up to have more impact on our community than people with Ph.D.s in inner-city studies or behavioral science. If you have a superiority complex, you are an enemy to your people. You're no higher or smarter than a sister who just got a GED and raised four kids with love and spirit.

There are very few people in the music business who I look up to. None really come to mind. There's Craig Hodges, the basketball player. Many leaders who were instrumental in the '60s, for lack of a better word, sold out. Some people who you thought were so upright, they'd be in it forever. But there are still some left in the struggle. These are the ones you don't see on TV or read about in books. They're the ones I look up to.

Afrikans are a powerful people, but peaceful. Dr. Livingstone came from Europe to observe African society. He said there were no jails. No rape. People would leave goods at the market overnight and no one would take them.

One difference between Afrikan and European culture is art. In Europe, art is separate from culture, abstract, an expression of the individual. Afrikan art was functional. People buy Afrikan masks and hang them on their walls. That's missing the point. The beads had stories. People would carve their entire family history on their walls. Art wasn't just the expression of the individual, it was a representation of the people.

Afrikan manhood and womanhood was developed as a cradle to the grave process. These were the most developed personalities in the history of the world. Europeans have all these technical toys but no human development. Because of the Disaster, we were forced to embrace a completely different kind of manhood and womanhood, the European kind which is individualistic as opposed to the Afrikan system of collectivity. That's why black children in fourth grade lose interest in American schools. It's like teaching a lion to be a goat. It doesn't work.

I used to sell rhinestone hats on the street fifteen to sixteen hours a day just to pay off the $500 phone bills I would have from calling record companies in New York. I'll never do that again. The music I'm making now record companies aren't gonna be too interested in anyway. But I don't need them either. I have a nice apartment. I'm respected in the community I live in. And I have a beautiful woman who I plan on marrying.

The industry isn't the place for something that's too focused. Take Paris. Paris is a powerful rapper. I've got a lot of respect for him as an artist. But your music should express a direction. His solution is to pick up a gun. What about after the gun stops smoking? Do we want to live in a society where black folks treat each other like white folks who taught us treat us?

Me and Cashus D just got together in 1990 and decided we needed to do something; Geoffrey Watts was instrumental also. We got with a lot of the rappers we knew and decided we needed to start one group to use hip-hop as a vehicle for positive change in the community.

We found out what artists' needs were. Someone would need a DJ, and we even held a writers workshop. The meetings occurred twice a month. It was dancers, graffiti artists, R&B singers, DJs, producers, but the majority was rappers. It was all brothers and sisters there, but that's not out of prejudice, but because black people have been the most exploited and when you talk about making a positive change in the black community, that can only come from black people. We offered a forum for brothers and sisters to address the problems they face in the music industry, and we were able to develop realistic solutions. Simple things, like how to prepare a demo package.

The reason the New World Order didn't work, we weren't prepared to do anything for the long-term so when things didn't happen as fast as we had expected, the membership started to dwindle. We started with about 50 people. We grew to 120. Then we diminished to about 20 over the next year. That's when we disbanded.

The mistakes I see:

1. We were very young and not prepared in leadership. We mobilized very well, but we weren't prepared to organize. In an ideal situation, each week there would be different workshops and training programs on public speaking, developing a package, how to conduct group sessions, mailing lists, etc. Instead we got together and just talked, and came up with solutions. We didn't set up nothing for brothers and sisters to implement the solutions.

2. The leadership was based on me and Cashus, so whatever we did, it would effect the whole group. There was no system set up to develop leaders. In a real organization, the leaders are just the spokespeople. They have no more authority than anyone else. They just have more administrative duties. If it's based on individual leadership, then it's destined to fail.

3. People were expecting overnight success. Participants were not committed enough to look for long-term benefits.

Rappers in Chicago right now need to be developing an organization that is based on collective leadership that will act as a protection for artists against the evils of the industry. It could start with the leaders from each organization again: Chi-Rock, Zulu, Dem Dare, Ill-State, Common Sense's crew. Suppose they were all pissed off about more rappers not getting signed out of Chicago. Then they could build a coalition around the issue. The problem is, once you get three or four rappers signed and they blow up, then the coalition is through. I mean *dogs* can meet around an issue. One big dog is bullying up on all the little dogs so the little dogs form a coalition to go kick his ass.

Dogs can't build an organization which has a protracted mission and is based on principles. That's what we need.

RENEGADES OF HIP-HOP

I keep trying to imagine what Afrika Bambaataa and them were thinking about when they invented hip-hop. What were they trying to get to? What were they trying to get away from? Take Afrika Bambaataa's breakthrough song "The Renegades of Funk." The Renegades of Funk! (A renegade is "a deserter, a turncoat.")

Here he was, Afrika Bambaataa, the godfather of hip-hop, creating one of hip-hop's pioneering anthems. It could have been called "The Pioneers of Hip-hop." But he didn't really see that yet. He saw what he was doing not as a completely new thing—hip-hop—but as a progression of the music he grew up on: funk. He was deserting it yes, he was breaking away from it yes, he was a renegade yes, but most of all, he was part of it.

Two decades later, hip-hop is the music of our time. No one has yet made a song called "The Renegades of Hip-hop." We who are part of hip-hop are supposed to have this unquestioning allegiance to it. Hip-hop has turned in on itself. We've gone from Whiz Kid and G.L.O.B.E.'s 1983 "Play that Beat Mr. DJ" talking about:

HIP-HOP

Punk rock, new wave and soul
Pop music, salsa, rock and roll
Calypso, Reggae, rhythm and blues
Master mix those number one tunes

to Lords of the Underground's 1993 response:

I got too much soul, rhythm and blues
R and B ya see all that's cool
But hip-hop and rap, yeah that's where my heart's at.

We say we are trying to preserve real hip-hop. We b-boy even though we can't make a living at it. We paint trains even though they don't run. We throw our effort into maintaining a culture we learned from the New York City of the 1970s and early '80s. Why? To preserve our childhoods? We are not children anymore. Hip-hop was not created to be preserved like a museum exhibit.

Graffiti is nothing but a medium of communication. It should never have become a subculture unto itself. It should never have become as predictable and dead and unexpressive as it is now. B-boying should never have become ghettoized and declared separate from any other form of dance. A hip-hop DJ was never meant to play only rap records. And MCing was never meant to be anything more than the effective use of language, sound, and a crowd—not the circus of categories it has become today.

Whatever else we try to make of it, hip-hop at its core is four forms of expression, nothing more. The best way for us now to show our respect for hip-hop is to move beyond it. Not in an arrogant way, saying that hip-hop is played out, or that we are "Post Hip-hop Nation" (the motto of Cross Colours).

VICTOR SAVOLAINEN

RAPPERS

94

No, The Next Great Thing isn't going to happen by someone ironing a phrase on a t-shirt, or sitting back in a room brainstorming. Superficial movements happen that way but not the important ones. Important movements happen because there is a void in our lives that demands to be filled. Hip-hop leaves voids all over the place.

One of the genuine voids in hip-hop is that it has no politics of its own. Many have tried to insert a politics into hip-hop. Whether it's the black nationalism of Public Enemy, the leftism of Disposable Heroes, the conservatism of TRQ, the feminism of Latifah, or one of the other thin, poster-board belief systems handed down to us from the 1960s, it's easy to see why hip-hop itself refuses to bow down for any of them.

Look at politics like it was music.

"I'm into making music that *never* could have been made by musicians," says DJ Scribe of New York. "To me, the creative part of hip-hop production is to take music from different genres, different time periods, different styles, and to fuse them into a new piece of music, a new whole—something distinct from the sum of its parts—something with a soul all its own.

"I'm opposed to taking more than one sample from the same song. But what's even worse is to loop an old R&B hit and put a new beat over it; of course it's going to be a hit again—there's no challenge. Not that I won't sample something recognizable in order to pay homage. But I don't abuse it. A lot of the people I sample would never even be able to recognize their own stuff."

And why stop with music? Music is only a small part of life. The attitude of the hip-hop DJ applies to other areas of life as well: Money, government, sex, violence, religion . . . When forming our outlook on any subject, we should be sampling sensible ideas from different groups, different time periods, different experiences, and fusing them into a new outlook, a new whole—something distinct from the sum of its parts—something with a soul all its own.

Bambaataa already got us searching "for the perfect beat." Why shouldn't we be searching for the perfect self, the perfect religion, the perfect economics, the perfect politics and law, the perfect science, the perfect society? Why shouldn't we be every bit as versatile with dusty ideas in those areas as Bambaataa is with dusty records—and every bit as selective.

An Interview with Wendy Day
THE COOLEST JOB IN THE WORLD

I put Wendy Day in a category that I don't put myself in: Wendy is a white person in hip-hop who I could stand to see more of. She's one of the few decent people in the music industry period. In March '92, she quit her corporate job and with her own money formed The Rap Coalition, a New York-based not-for-profit organization designed to serve and protect rap artists at no charge to them. "I have the coolest job in the world," she says. "As long as rappers are getting screwed, I'm here for 'em."

WENDY: I read the "Autobiography of Malcolm X." That's what started everything. I remember I found it hard to believe that there could be a black person who hated white people so much. It opened a huge door for me. He was based on love of his own people, not on hate of others. I started reading the books Malcolm X said he read in prison. I was like 20. I was a white girl from the Philly suburbs. The only person I knew who was listening to rap. Everyone else was listening to Led Zeppelin, the Cars.

I was a huge yuppie. I had money out the ass. I had a new BMW at the age of 25 that I bought myself. I was living in a quarter-million-dollar house. I ate every meal in restaurants. I had a husband. I had everything I was supposed to want, except I wasn't happy. In fact, I was miserable. I was reading as much to escape as for knowledge. I found out it wasn't fun to make and spend money. I decided to quit my job and come back to New York. I originally moved to New York from Philly in 1986. I'm embarrassed to tell you why. There was this radio show Friday nights on WBLS with Mr. Magic and Marley Marl . . . I had lived in New York in '88. The father of one of my friends had this liquor company in Montreal.

He said, I want you to come run my company.

I laughed and said, You couldn't afford me.

He said, How much?

I told him. He said okay, he even raised me $20,000. I packed, got married, and started running the company within five days. As you can tell, I'm very impulsive.

So after I quit at the liquor company, I came back to New York and took the summer off. It was the first time since 16 when I didn't have to work. I was just really a rap fan. I wasn't thinking about doing it for a living. I was a huge RUN-DMC fan. When I bought my BMW, I got RUN-DMC license plates. I had to try five states to get them. Finally they let me do it in Delaware. I had to change my legal residence to Delaware to get the plates.

During my summer off, I took this class at the New School with Bert Padell. Bert had a huge influence on me. He manages Madonna, Robert DeNiro, Eric B, Rakim, Al B. Sure, etc. etc. I realized, wow, I could work in the music business.

It happened to be the same year a bunch of shit happened. Eric B and Rakim got screwed. X-Clan got screwed. Sir-Mix-A-Lot got screwed. Puffy did a basketball game where people got crushed to death and the media lynched him for it. That pissed me off, but what pissed me off more was that nobody except Heavy D stepped to his defense. They all just sort of took it.

I went to Bert. I said What the fuck is up with this?

He said It sucks but that's the way it is.

I went home literally that night and in eight hours I wrote this proposal for The Rap Coalition. Came up with the name and everything. Sold my BMW and started the company. I called Russell Simmons every day for 4 months trying to get information and advice. It was a joke. He never took my calls. I called David Mays at *The Source* every day for like two months. I irritated him. Finally he talked to me. He was very helpful. He said I don't have time to help but here are the needs.

Once I got really into it, I heard more horror stories of kids getting screwed. The main reason they were getting screwed was because they didn't have access to good lawyers—which were almost always the most expensive lawyers. Talking to a lot of up-and-coming rappers, they had a very low opinion of lawyers. It was a whole different world to them. I knew I had the ability to travel in both worlds, so I set myself up as a go-between. I met with

DEEP

the most powerful lawyers in the industry. They already had more money than God. Some of them agreed to do it pro bono.

The record companies are not run like any business on the face of this Earth. They piss away money. Coming from corporate America, it was shocking. They're not run like IBM or Xerox. If they were, they'd have like twelve times as much money as they have now and they'd be controlling the US economy. It's amazing how poorly they're run! I'm really generalizing at this point. I was still taking Bert Padell's course. I took it five semesters in a row. That's where I get my best ideas.

It's amazing how much need there is for what I do. I'm working twenty hour days, seven days a week. I could keep doing this for one hundredyears and not even make a dent. That's how much exploitation there is. A friend of mine gave me a tape of this group called the Kemelions from Long Island. I popped it into my tape deck. I had been doing Rap Coalition for six to eight months. I was living, sleeping, breathing, rap. I read every book that had to do with the music industry. I was going to every event with the letter *R* in it.

When I listened to the Kemelions, I thought they were one of the most brilliant groups. Kind of like Tribe, but with the social awareness of PE. They had a CD called Basement Arrangements. Absolutely brilliant. I said Why haven't I heard of these guys before? How come they never perform? How come I never read about them? I called the label and they barely knew who they were. I spoke to a knucklehead publicist. He told me they were from Long Island. I got the number of this guy in the group, Poepan. I called him out of the blue.

I said ,I love your shit, what's up with the company? He just broke down and started to tell me what he had suffered in the music industry. They started out on Jazzy Jay's label and got screwed big time. Then they got signed to Island. Island did nothing with them. They just sat there. Then they were signed to Zoo by Lou Maglia. He used to be the guy who ran 4th and Broadway when they fucked Eric B and Rakim. My eyes got the size of Eddie Murphy eyes.

I contacted Lou Maglia. I said, What are you doing with the Kemelions? I pressured him into doing something. He said he'd put out a single. All they had was an EP which they didn't promote. It sold some units anyway. Underground DJs around the country played it. This writer for *The Source* named Ricaldo was behind it. I pumped it myself. I called a lot of radio stations. I introduced them to Grandmaster Flash who agreed to re-mix their single for free. A year later, the single still hasn't come out. I wanted to pull them off the label but

RAPPERS

98

they thought Lou could do something for them. It's a slow, uphill struggle.

There's an artist in Orlando, DJ Magic Mike. He owns a record label called Magic Records. He has kids write or produce albums. He gets them to sign over all their publishing. He tells them he's going to put out their album and then he doesn't. I helped get one artist off the label named Smooth J. Smoothe. He was so anxious to get off, he took the first deal Mike made, he walked away from five songs, two of which are on a gold album. Then another guy from Orlando called me because he heard I could get people off the label. We're suing Magic Mike for breach of contract.

Rap Coalition does more than sue. We act as a watchdog for injustices. For example, you see ads in rap magazines for compilation albums. You call this number in Beaumont TX. or Arkansas. You pay $1,500 and they're supposed to send twenty thousand copies to every A&R in the country. First of all, if your goal is to get heard, they almost never work. Nobody listens to compilation albums.

None of the old-schoolers own their own publishing—up until the early KRS-ONE. They don't own their own music! That really makes me sick. Grandmaster Flash doesn't own "The Message." Sylvia Robinson owns it. So every time Ice Cube's song is played—"Check-ity Check Yourself . . ." Sylvia Robinson gets paid. That pissed me off and Flash is on my Board of Directors. I assume the best of people so I assumed Cube didn't know and I wrote him a letter. If he'd known, he could have called Flash and asked him if he could make a new song that sounds similar to the Message, so Flash could get paid too when the shit goes platinum.

I adamantly refuse to charge the artists for the services I provide. They've been ganked so badly by the time they end up here. I want to restore their faith in human nature as I help them! Most come to me as a last resort. They have no money and they need to get off a label. A lot of them don't read these books about the industry. They're raised in an environment where

NIKOLE COOK

reading was never pushed. I have degrees out my ass and I still can't read a lot of these books. The best book is Donald Passman's *All You Need to Know About The Music Business*. It's the best $25 somebody will ever spend. I've even bought the book for people. People who have trouble getting a buck twenty-five to come into the city to see me. Here. Read this.

These cases are not well-publicized. Artists don't talk about how they're getting screwed. It's a combination of them not talking and nobody listening. There needs to be a publication set up for this. I've been working on a newsletter since October. There's too much info in it. I can't afford to send it out. I'm frustrated. The problem with being this busy is that I don't have enough time to devote to my freelance (income-producing) work and it's fucking me financially. I must figure out a good way to finance what I'm doing 'cause I'm most valuable when I'm helping rappers.

I'm an organizer. I have the ability to see a need and fill it. It's rare that rappers call each other and say, "Do you see that this is going on? What are we going to do about it?" But I can call both of them and get them together. We're in the process of forming a union. There's people in management, law, publicity. One person from Zulu Nation. We got a list from Washington of what you have to do to become a union. It's not realistic for hip-hop. It would have to be a lot looser than a regular union and without the corruption. Rap Coalition already acts as a sort of rap union.

I usually deal with the negative. There are a lot of good people in power. Bill Stephney who runs Step Sun Records. Queen Latifah. Deborah Mannis at Diamondtime Sample Clearing House. She called up Farrakhan to clear a sample and he said, I don't know what's a fair price. She gave him a fair price. The Stop the Violence campaign was a ray of hope. Karen Mason is a ray of hope. We need to put the positive, trustworthy folks in positions of power. Pepper Johnson's basketball games. Sheena Lester, the editor of *Rappages* is a huge beacon of hope. The attitudes of artists are very bright even though they get taken advantage of. To help somebody help themselves is the most amazing feeling. Better than sex. If you've never had that feeling, it's unexplainable.

Why don't more people do what you're doing?
Because there's no money in altruism. Ha! It's a dying art. I don't even want to do this for the rest of my life. I'd like to see Rap Coali-

tion running itself in about five years as a membership organization with a board. I just want to build it and make it work. I'd like to make some money again. This being poor sucks. I can't remember the last time I went shopping. That used to be my favorite thing. I haven't taken time off in two years. But as much as I complain about money, I've never been so happy. My family sees how happy I am. Everyone sees it. I see it.

Like where do you get off thinking it's your place to do what you're doing?
Because I care as a human being.

What about hip-hop's potential to change society?
I think it influences people but it's more of a superficial thing. I don't see people going and organizing because they heard a rap record. Take the protest of Calvin Butts. That came from myself, Preacher Earl, and a marketing company who was using it as a publicity stunt. I could count on my hand the number of people from the rap community who were there. Artists are too busy with their careers and their own lives.

What about Zulu?
Well, Zulu is wonderful. There was a gang summit in New York recently. Zulu showed up four hundred deep. That's pretty fuckin impressive. I'm sure it scares the cops. I'm a member of Zulu. They have meetings every Wednesday night, but I don't see anything earthshattering coming out of their meetings. Harry Allen, he's another bright spot. He really wants to help the Zulu Nation become a force.

I have to think about this hip-hop-as-a-social-movement . . . In a way, I want it. In a way it would scare the hell out of me. Rap is so mismanaged, so misrun. There's no unity. That would really fuck up a revolution.

But hip-hop's still so new. It'll evolve. I think it's in its infancy stage. It just became super-exploitable within the last two to four years which in the scale of things is a very short time.

MARGARITA GARCIA

A guided tour through one of Chicago's best kept secrets

THE URBAN FRONTIER

The next tour begins in five minutes.

I have a simple question for anyone who thinks they know Chicago; bite your lip. What is there to do or to see—in the nearly two mile stretch—between Chinatown and Downtown?

That area? I've driven by there a million times. Some old factories and railroad tracks, that's about it. No one goes around that area; it's completely abandoned.

My own early education about the near South Side came from my father. My father used to tell the story of this small-town family from somewhere in the Midwest who, after finishing dinner at a restaurant in Chinatown, decided to work off the meal by walking back to their downtown hotel. Not knowing what kind of neighborhoods lay in their path, the bumpkins aimed for the skyline and started walking. Within a few blocks, daddy bumpkin was found dead on the sidewalk.

Horror stories like this one—told with an underlying sense of smugness at knowing, unlike someone from out-of-town, that there are poor black (pronounced "high-crime") neighborhoods around Chinatown—encourage children of the urban bourgeoisie to confine their lives, like the lives of their parents, to the sliver of upscale territory along the lakefront or to the outskirts of town. Through generations of urban bourgeoisie wisdom, "street smart" has come to mean knowing which half of Chicago not to visit. But what can a person who fears his own city presume to know of the world?

If your impressions of the area were like mine, perhaps it sounds absurd to be told that this desolate, probably dangerous, stretch of Earth between these two familiar "towns" is worthy of a guided tour—which begins in four minutes.

Imagine a vast abandoned land—spanning an area of about twenty-five city blocks in all—a composite of forest, prairie, and urban archaeological dig. Wild rabbits and pheasants live here. At least a dozen city streets find their dead ends along its perimeter. And with increasing land commercialization, it is one of the decaying places at the heart of our city *which have inherited* one of the most sacred roles in the experience of our nation, that of the frontier. The urban frontier.

Today, as the cityscape gags and doubles over on mini-malls and cable TV wires, and as an increasing number of city kids can't afford to "Escape to Wisconsin" or anywhere really, the urban frontier is uniquely situated to grab hold of today's young imagination, claiming for its own the romance which once belonged to the Old West.

Even among those who can afford to escape the city, the urban frontier holds a certain attraction. It has no tawdry gift shops, no concession stands, no trailer parks. Deep down, most of us want more out of our vacations than the sterility of theme parks, resorts, and well-traveled wilderness. Even risky ventures like skydiving still keep us safe from what we fear most of all, which is of course the other half of our own city—the half where *The Chicago Reader* isn't available.

The urban frontier, where raw city meets raw wilderness, is an antidote to the incompleteness of the segregated city life. For the sheltered bourgeoisie, it means an introduction to the forbidden urban underworld. For the sheltered poor, it means an introduction to the unfamiliar natural habitat. For all, it exists more than anything as a frontier of the mind, a living monument to the deepest fears and fascinations of a segregated city.

Alas, it is simple adventure, simple crossing of barriers or frontiers, that dull children from sheltered lives really yearn for when they turn to Nintendo, Great America or the latest craze in commercially packaged entertainment. The forbidden domains of the city are where the real adventure lies. The greatest opportunities in the world to explore the unknown, meet amazing people, and become cosmopolitan cost only a CTA token. So send the children across the sea; send them off to college. The tour begins in three minutes.

Despite its central location in the city, the twenty-five-square-block piece of land I've been talking about is so ignored that no one even knows what to call it. Hell, I don't even know what to call it. Usually, people speak of it (if they bother to mention it at all) in relation to what it's between (the Loop and Chinatown, east of the river, west of Clark Street)—or in relation to where they were going before they got lost in it. *The Chicago Tribune* has called it "the generally blighted strip . . . [full of] weed-filled vacant lots and exposed, underused, railroad track." I'll just say it's the frontier because that's what uncharted lands have always been called.

You don't have to be a boy to go there. My friend Liz isn't a boy and she goes there. Liz goes everywhere. Liz thinks the entire conventional wisdom about crime in America is baloney. "I go to the ghetto all the time," shrugs the 17-year-old blond. "The only thing that scares me is the burnt-out buildings. They're like the real monsters. People are people. I don't understand the paranoia."

"Well, I did sort of get stabbed one time," she adds hesitantly. "It was a couple years ago. I thought the police were chasing me on the El, so I hopped off on Indiana [station at 40th street] and ran down this alley. These boys started following me. I had just got these new gym shoes—these Air Jordan's—and they said 'give us your shoes.' So I say, No, what am I going to wear? And then one of them comes up behind me, I guess he had a knife, and he gets me in my back, and I started yelling at them, and I took off my gym shoes and threw them at them. I said, Take my fuckin shoes! Then they kind of got scared and ran away. I got back on the train and went home."

After that, Liz learned her lesson: "I'll never get an expensive pair of shoes like that again! The stab wasn't that bad . . . I hope my mom doesn't read this. She already doesn't like me taking the CTA on the South Side at night . . ."

In truth, Chicago has many frontiers; this one on the Near South Side is only my favorite. Everywhere train tracks, water, factories, parks, rooftops—or just plain neglect—conspire to create secret places within the city. It is possible to pass these places, to look down on them from an overpass or from the window of a commuter train, but the real luxury is in being here on foot, in having the freedom to roam the land indefinitely, to stop and start, to rest and climb, whenever and wherever you feel like it. I feel an affection for this frontier now, but originally I came for the most ordinary of reasons. I wanted to see what was over here.

The area was created during the '20s and '30s during two stages. From 1925–37, the city vacated more than nine square blocks south of 16th, between Wentworth and the Chicago River for rail yards, and at about the same time passed an ordinance to straighten out the river where it snaked east between 10th street and 18th, pushing it a block-and-a-half west of its original location. Midcentury, the railroad business collapsed and a huge strip of wilderness was left to sprout. On paper at least, this land has been carved up by developers, but they haven't built much yet because there are no utilities, phone wires, streets or sewers on the land.

I guess by now you're getting impatient. Okay, let the tour begin. My directions may not be safe, but then again do I look to you like the Surgeon General?

Get off the Dan Ryan El at 22nd/Cermak station which is one block east of Chinatown; turn right at the miniature pagoda on Wentworth, as though you were going to the Chinatown parking lot. Instead of entering the lot, gentle readers, continue walking back toward downtown.

Haunted music please. As you cross Archer Avenue, you have already entered the ghost city. Tall, sinewy plants shoot up five feet through the suddenly patchy Wentworth, a street which dead-ends, after ten miles of grandeur, on the next block. On your right, Dan

Ryan tracks plunge into the ground where it is said they will one day connect with the Howard line, and on the left abandoned buildings offer a humble welcome. If you see people on this street, your drinking problem is serious.

The first building is an old, freshly boarded-up, two-story red brick train commissary station. The station's facade appears tidily swept most of the time, probably a courtesy of the wind. Contractors are erecting a shopping mall along Archer just inside the southern edge of the great land. How do you like that? You haven't even gotten to the frontier yet and already it's shrinking.

A block behind you stands the gateway to Chinatown; before you, temporarily at least, stands the gateway to the frontier. Spray-painted tag names sprinkle lampposts, crumbling buildings, and every nearby surface. The names are concentrated here because of the nearby graffiti Wall of Fame. Barbed-wire construction fence flanks the train station on both sides, but there is a hole in between the fence and the next building—a torched and abandoned truck loading dock—a hole that the average-sized person should have no trouble slipping through.

(If the hole in the fence is patched, which happens periodically, you can also enter where Wentworth dead-ends at the base of the 18th street bridge, or hell, you could just hop the fence—but beware, the construction site on Archer has 24-hour security.)

As you cross the threshold of the abandoned loading dock, your thoughts race back in time to the stories of childhood. Stories of adventurous children who dared to explore the house on the hill; deep sea divers who rummage a phantom shipwreck; astronauts who piece through the ruins of an extraterrestrial civilization.

Lucky for new-jack explorers, the loading dock isn't too creepy, at least not as abandoned buildings go. Although the outer shell remains mostly intact, there are enough openings to let in light. A sea of bricks, cinders, beams, glass, plaster, insulation, and tile layers the floor. Scale what remains of the stairway up to the curious accordion-like fixtures on the second floor—if you can manage to get up there without falling through the stairwell—and to the third floor, where a ladder leads to the roof.

At times it's hard to discern what has been scorched by fire, rusted out, or just dumped here. In the center of the main room, a hole has been smashed into the cellar; doorways lead into side rooms. Graffiti seems to lurk like giant spiders. I dare anyone to climb that roof at night. (1991)

WARP'S LEGACY AND MY STUPID ONE

When I first happened upon the frontier (I spied it from the window of a Dan Ryan El train) I was a 13-year-old graffiti writer and the area had no graffiti. Hmm, I thought, biting my lip.

At that time, Chicago graffiti writers—when they weren't doing actual trains and buses—devoted most of their energy to painting rooftops along CTA train lines. Then, in 1987, the book *Spray Can Art* helped to popularize the idea of the "graffiti art gallery": An abandoned set of walls where we could paint even during the daytime with little fear of being chased, arrested, electrocuted, hit by a train, or confusing colors in the dark. A place without disturbance, a play without audience, a gallery of laziness to do your art.

By 1989, the area centered around the 18th Street railroad and river underpass—known to graffiti writers as the Wall of Fame or "Fame" for short—with sister walls springing up at 12th and 16th streets had become the most graffiti saturated section of the city. Every inch that could be reached by standing on or climbing something had been painted and painted again—even the rafters crossing above the river were crowded with tags.

(The 1991 *Chicago Tribune* story on graffiti neglected to mention the Wall of Fame among the city's "fiercest zones." But hey, when you're writing about something as subterranean as graffiti, who's going to notice if most of your research and photographs haven't been current since 1986? It wasn't until the *Trib's* 1994 magazine story that the Fame was finally discovered in the mainstream press—on 18th & Damen, a mere seventeen blocks from its actual location.)

Even for someone who has personally contributed to the painting, I found myself perplexed to see so much graffiti in such an abandoned place. Mental equation: here is graffiti; people write graffiti; where are the people? It was the juxtaposition of evident effects with invisible causes which created the feeling of disbelief. Like waking up in a strange blanket when nobody else was home.

A fellow graffiti writer once confessed he sometimes felt as though the people who wrote all the graffiti down here were going to jump out and surround him.

"But you know all these people," I protested. Most Chicago graffiti writers used to know each other.

"But still," he said. "It just feels that way. It makes my skin crawl, like the place is infested or something. It feels lawless, like it's some kind of a gang headquarters." A while later he asked me suddenly and in a disturbed tone if I'd read a book called *Lord of the Flies.*

By 1991, the Wall of Fame stood a sad monument to youth culture gone ugly. Although pieces were still painted here weekly, they were destroyed within days by scribbling idiots. Away from the fame, pieces fared better. These are the jewels in the belly of the city, the gold in the river of the urban frontier. A message left on a nearby wall from one writer to another: "To Antck, this spot is still hush hush." Zore even thought to include beside his piece a built-in space for taggers with a simple request: "If you must tag, do it here, not on our piece."

That saved the piece for about a week.

It had become the Wall of Shame. I was even ashamed of it. Shorties would come up to me. "You started the Wall of Fame?" I'd be, "Yeah, don't paint there. It was the worst mistake I ever made." Tyke, Ages, Fred, Deep, and Nike fucked up by popularizing throwups in Chicago. Ian fucked up with scratch-bombing. Seven years later, I look back on my misguided little monster. How many thousands of cans were wasted down here? How many pieces lie trapped under the layers? How many battles were fought over walls that would be gone over anyway within the week? Now Chicago has a hundred wall of fames. I'm ashamed of all of them.

During the heyday of the original Fame in 1988-89, upwards of eighty kids would show up on Saturday mornings for the all-city writers meeting.

The highlight of each writers' meeting was afterwards when we would all stampede up the connector ramp to the nearby Chinatown El station. Sometimes the herd of us would even stop a train to cross the track, then board the same train once it arrived at the station. Then we'd ride all over the city getting on and off of trains, standing in between cars with our homemade two-inch markers, rocking everything—didn't care who saw us—and scaring all those nice, gentle people away from using public transportation.

One time, a writers' convention was interrupted by this goofy Cheech 'n' Chong motherfucker with his jumbo ziplock bag of marijuana to sell. Then this big fat Jheri-Kurl writer named Stash tried to grab the bag away from him. A fight ensued and the marijuana began to spill on the ground. Within moments, a dozen writers were scrambling around trying to pinch some of the fallen herb into their pockets. Meanwhile, the two were still fighting, all of this in plain daylight, no one trying to break it up.

The Wall of Fame meetings were only one in a series of all-city writers meetings held in different parts of the city. The first and some would say best of these was held in the fall of 1985 by a high school senior from Cabrini Green named Warp, the Afrika Bambaataa of Chicago graffiti.

WARP: Graffiti was becoming serious. It had brought together all these nationalities, all these backgrounds. I wanted to let it be understood that you have a force here. It was bigger than a cat-and-mouse chase. It was power. It's for us to have a say-so in what happens and what gets out to the public. We didn't have to go through channels. It's just like if Michael Jordan stood up and said, "Nobody go to work tomorrow." A lot of people wouldn't go to work. It was like "We've got the power. What are we going to do with it?"

A lot of the old-schoolers were in grammar school at the time. Being young, sometimes you can't take a step back and see everything from a distance. I was 18 going on 20. I had a little age on me that allowed me to see.

Subway Art wasn't out yet. It was almost like a new world. Something that had been needed that was missing. There was nothing vibrant going on. A lot of the youth that got into it at the beginning were into gangs. So it was replacing an ill.

I was hoping we would channel and harness this energy to see how to direct it, as opposed to letting it go all over like in New York. Chicago isn't New York. It's not as loose a city. We would have to be tighter, more strategically set-up as far as bombing, piecing, racking, bum-rushing. We didn't have the room to be sloppy.

ORKO: Me and Warp talked on the phone. I was saying, "How can we get trains to run?" He said, "We gotta unite and all paint at the same time. Yo cat, let's get organized and throw a meeting." It was the Olivet meeting. That was the name of the community center.

WARP: The Olivet is where I grew up all my life. I talked to the staff members there about having a meeting of a bunch of young artists. I called about eighty people myself. It was on a Saturday. That gave about two weeks. I didn't know how many people would show up. It was two hundred plus people. Everyone in GGC (Graffiti Groove Crew) had a role in getting people there as safely as possible. We didn't want anyone to get lost in Cabrini Green. The gangs there, they could see a bunch of Puerto Ricans rolling up and . . .

DEFSKI: Everybody knew about it. It was so cool. You were supposed to get off at Clark and Division, and there was a representative waiting to meet you there. It was pretty organized.

DEMO: I had to have been about 13. Warp had me, Tran, DJ Philgood, and Static going to pick people up from different stations.

DEFSKI: I think I could honestly say every crew was represented. It was like *The Warriors*. We wanted to bomb Chicago as much as New York was bombed. I remember I got up and said: We got to keep graffiti alive. We can't let it die like breakin'. And I remember Orko said: The police can kiss my Pentel!

ORKO: Every crew that came thought they were Number 1. It was just like The Warriors. Warp was like Cyrus, but he wasn't in full control. The meeting was about how we were going to do the trains

all in one night. They tuned into him for a second . . . word, word
. . .but was still tryna get Scarce to sign they piecebook.

Writers were mysterious back then. It was like going to Holly-
wood and meeting all the celebrities. It introduced all the major lea-
guers to each other, and it introduced them to the common people.
It was also a turning point for a lot of black writers because the
Latins were running it then. But it was Warp who got everybody to-
gether, and Trixter was just getting a position. I was on my way up.
We took account of how many black writers there was, and we said,
"We can do this."

It was a vision by Warp. He said we should all concentrate on
one line, the Howard Line, and that's what happened. The Howard
was the best line. It's always been the center of graffiti in Chicago.

DEMO: It was glorious, man. That could have been the start of
something big. It blew everybody's mind. If they would've really listened, we would've got a lot accomplished. Warp was talking
throughout the whole meeting, but after awhile only a certain bunch
of people was paying attention. He got sick of trying to talk to
everybody, saying "Listen up. Listen up." I maybe could've listened
a little harder myself.

Warp was on that international zone-coaster type stuff. He wanted to go in and grab maps of the tunnels and the lay-ups. If we'd a listened to Warp, we'd a had the city by the balls.

ORKO: Warp was trying to figure out who was from where—from
around which train yard—and trying to get people to meet each other.
We had to take the meeting outside into this lot because it was too
crowded. Warp was still speaking, and Hate [R.I.P.] wasn't tryna hear
it. Hate was ACW. That was the largest crew and Kre-8 had just died,
so he felt he had power. Hate said whoever wanna be in Cocaine
[crew] come over here. He *split* the meeting because then half the people went over with him. Once it separated, shit got outta line.

DEMO: Some people followed Hate across the street over to this
abandoned building.

ORKO: Tap wrote his name on this building. And then everybody
was like fuck it, we'll write our names too.

DEMO: They were coming back across the street to the meeting, and
the police were coming up behind them, but wasn't nobody gonna
run. Warp had talked to the police, told them we were just some
artists having a meeting. Then Hate looked around and yelled Police
and he hopped over a fence, and then everybody started running and

flipping fences.

DEFSKI: We were inside. We started freaking out because someone ran in and said that there was a raid. We all ran into the bathroom to hide our gear. I remember people were climbing up to hide their Magnums on the ceiling beams.

ORKO: Police swarmed the whole fucking meeting at the count of twenty. They came from everywhere. It was quite a mess. People was scattering, jumping gates, and cops was running up on curbs, grabbing people. Warp said "Why y'all running?" I'd say about thirty people ran, and the rest of us stood there with Warp. Those who ran got hooked-up. Some1 was standing there holding a can of spray paint. They took him to jail for being ignorant.

DEMO: It was pandemonium. Nobody knew where they was. A group of writers tried to hide in the abandoned building. The police went in there and writers got caught up. They came out to the paddy wagons, had spray paint on they face. Heads, lips busted open. Only a group of us stood there with Warp.

DEFSKI: After that meeting, Warp threw another meeting at the Golden Dome on the West Side. It was called the Golden Dome. It was actually the Garfield Park Conservatory. What those meetings gave us at a very early age was that, regardless of whether we had a space or not, we could organize. The scene was broken up back then by different sides of town. Not everybody knew what was going on but there was definitely more unity than today. People had their beefs. We were teenagers. But there was none of this shit, beating people up for going over people's shit. I was at a party recently, and I heard these writers talking about, "Yeah, I'm a beat the shit outta these guys," I was like, "What are you talking about?"

ORKO: I don't remember what the issues were at these meetings. The Lincoln Park meeting was another showboat meeting. Me and Trixter called it because we still had this crazy idea to get all these trains painted. We came wearing those Burger King crowns. We were trying to squash a lot of beefs. We tried to squash the Hate thing, but he really fucked up bad by splitting the meeting and getting everyone arrested.

Then there was the North-South war. Paint started that—he started a lot of wars. Me and Paint was doing sides at North & Clybourne, and the South Siders used to do them at 40th & Indiana. We seen one of Paint's trains come back with Paint's name crossed out by one of the same cans that was bombing on Indiana. So Paint crossed out the whole car, and wrote North Side. Then there were the South Side meetings on 40th and Indiana. I made that the South Side writers bench. The South Side writers would get together and bum-rush stores and act a fool. As Pause stood up and said: This meeting is for all of us to get together and take out all these toys who are tryna be king of our line. Fun [R.I.P.] said: Let's start with you. And that was the end of the meeting.

All these meetings were thrown to get some kind of organization to bomb the trains. But because of egos, rivalries, and dick-holding, Warp never got to talk like he wanted to. The only thing we all had in common were the trains.

In Chicago, graffiti is like an addiction, a religion. People were letting their father go, their brother go, and accepting Warp as their big brother. New York and Chicago was where it was kids in the ghetto giving their art for the people in the projects to see and maybe live a couple more days. I don't even think we cared about parties or girls. In Chicago it was a family. We got together to bomb. It was a culture. Those were the days that turned me into a writer, that turned P-Lee into a DJ and Stane into a rapper on Jamalski's album.

The culture is gone. Chicago lost their identity. People who were in the fore left. They got tired of tolerating the bullshit. Your major people quit by 1988. Now it's all people tryna get permission walls and imitate California with all the fancy doodle-letters that make no sense. They didn't hang around a lot in the projects and on the trains so they don't even know what hip-hop is about. If you didn't hang out in the projects or on the trains you ain't hip-hop. Graffiti is the center of hip-hop. That's why everybody wants to pose in front of graffiti for their albums. That's why the best MCs were all graffiti writers. KRS-ONE. Rakim.

If I had it to do again, I would've had two meetings. I would have a primary meeting to bring together the presidents of all major crews before the big meeting so if a crew member got out of line, there would be someone there to tell them to shut up. All the meetings had good intentions but they never went as planned. Crazy Man broke up our meeting at Lincoln Park. He was crazy. He did a dive into the bushes, then he swan-dived into a garbage can.

FANTOM: Crazy Man ran out in the middle of the street in front of a bus, stopped the bus and started licking the front window to distract the driver. We all ran up to the side of the bus and started bombing it. There was at least about twenty of us. We were fighting for space. (WITH RESEARCH BY THE *SUBWAY AND ELEVATED* STAFF)

WHY CHICAGO IS THE ONLY PLACE THAT HAS ALL-CITY HIP-HOP MEETINGS

I grew up thinking every city had writers' meetings like we had. They don't. LA has never had an all-city writers' meeting. Neither has New York.

CRAZY LEGS (NYC): All-city meetings? What are those? All-city writers meetings? No. Nothing like that happens here on the regular. I think people been watching too much *Warriors* and *Beat Street*. We have our own personal shit to worry about. It ain't about no "Let's have a mass graffiti meeting." What's the purpose of it? Do you know the purpose? I mean brothers can't even get their own shit together. How are they gonna help other people? Some people can. I'm not talking about everyone. But I don't know what these meetings you got out there are gonna do.

You got to remember people out here had their own little posses, getting together their portfolios, opening storefronts. It's about "I got $300, you got $300, he's got $300. Let's all get together and make a clothing line and have only graffiti writers do it." I'm down for that. But that takes sacrificing. That's different from just going to a meeting and talking about the same old thing over and over again. And half of the people are smoking blunts and drinking 40s . . . Can you really do business like that?

Other cities had meetings but they lacked even a sense of purpose.
ARI: In Philadelphia, the meetings were about everybody meeting each other, getting fucked-up, writing and fighting. Usually about forty people would show-up. Never more than about sixty or seventy, and that was on a good day. There wasn't no plans of "let's all bomb here," or something. Organization? No, the only organization

we had was when we would put all our money together to get some wine and 40s. They ended in '85 because people kept snitching and we kept getting raided by the Anti-Graffiti Network.

ORKO: In San Francisco, graffiti is like jogging. It's like an art class. It's just ridiculous. It's all based on crews out here. People stick to their own neighborhood and don't mingle. Most crews are to they-self. People who are into your KRS-ONE are not going to listen to Too Short. New people don't even care who the old people are. Taggers don't care about pieces. Hip-hop is distorted. People go their separate ways.

The first big meeting was thrown by Krayone. About three hundred people came. It was all to bring attention to his crew. (It turned into a rivalry between new wave style, drawing robots and shit like it was an art class, versus the ghetto style which was focused around letters which was wildly influenced by me coming out here from Chicago.) There wasn't a cause behind it. I don't know what it was about. Krayone didn't speak at all. Everybody was into they own thing. Even the toys had their own crowd. They wasn't mixing in.

A lot of people don't think much of the Chicago meetings either.
ANONYMOUS: When I first started writing, people went to meetings to just be in a big group then walk around and bumrush stores or write or whatever. Basically, it was "Hi, I'm a writer too." They were lonely or something. I don't know why we had meetings. I have no idea really, now that I think about it. I really don't remember anything productive that came out of them. They were basically just stupid. I think the whole idea was idiotic, unless you wanted to be surrounded by police. It was like a turkey shoot.

Other cities would laugh at the idea of having all-city meetings. There's nothing to be solved by having a town meeting. There are too many differences. I'd rather go home and read a book. Countless times you hear stupid things like "you think I should flip him?" . . . "word, I'm gonna start flipping him." Or people talk about things they don't know about, filling in the blanks from what they heard from someone else. I think Chicago hasn't figured out that it's a stupid idea yet.

But the people who criticize the all-city writers' meetings haven't been to one in a while, and they don't really know what they're talking about. First of all, they aren't just writers' meetings anymore. In the summer of 1986, on the South Side, a rapper named Kingdom called the first all-city rap meeting.

KINGDOM: I was tryna get a Battle Royale going with a lot of rappers from different parts of the city. Me and JMD called the meeting at Stagg Stadium. There would be forty to fifty people. We would have them at night. Incognito. We would hop over the fence.

The idea of hip-hop meetings I'm not going to take credit for. Me and Artistic used to go to school together at Dunbar. Artistic wanted to have an all-city graffiti meeting, and I wanted to have a rap meeting. Then I remember hearing on WHPK about a hip-hop meeting in Grant Park. That was supposed to be for everybody. By '90, we were having regular hip-hop meetings.

Now we take it for granted that there's hip-hop all over the city. Before, it was like a blessing to meet another hip-hopper. You could say we were the grassroots, trying to organize Chicago hip-hop back then. We were there for each other. Like with DA at the Regal, we went out in a blizzard, in the cold for hours, to support him and help him get his money back. Anyone who was known and did their work in hip-hop could call a meeting about anything and people would come out to support.

The all-city hip-hop meetings, which became synonymous with Chi-Rock meetings, have come a long way in the last year organizationally, but they have begun to look more and more like a giant clique than an all-city meeting. One meeting recently began promptly only ten minutes after it was supposed to start. Fifty or so Chi-Rock members sat cross-legged around a large circle, several of them taking notes. The meeting ran on an agenda, with breaking and rhyming intermissions. The discussion, focused and practical, included little of the usual interruptions, and "I've gotta get this off my chest" speechmaking which characterizes most early attempts to organize. Then at the next meeting no one showed up.

SHANE, 38, THE GREAT AMERICAN HOMESTEADER

There isn't much in the way of human life on the frontier, but four enterprising homesteaders, subtracting themselves from the homeless, have set up camp here—not many considering how many people are living in Grant Park these days. At the suggestion they could have more privacy if they moved around here, the Grant Park tramps have been quick to tell me they would be too scared to live in such an abandoned place. City kids.

"I feel much safer sleeping out here [in downtown] where at least the cops will come by if someone tries to kill you in your sleep," explained a man who survives by washing car windows. "If you get in trouble and you're all alone out there—not close to any busy streets—no one is going to help you out."

Shane Wilson, a crippled but sturdy man of 38 doesn't need anyone's help. Three years ago, Shane built himself a one-room house on the frontier, tucked away in a grove of trees, and he has lived there with his two dogs ever since. (The dogs are free to roam the city and forage for food, but they always return home.)

On a hot afternoon in August, he leans forward on his one-chair porch with small, near-sighted eyes focused calmly from behind round spectacles. He wears a camouflage bush hat over a patchy brown face; sweatshirt open at the chest; a pair of cutoff jeans and black high-tops like stables into which are stuck his skinny bare ankles.

"I like it here," Shane begins, speaking strictly in abrupt sentences, "because I'm scared of everybody—'cause I'm a paranoid son of a bitch." Intently silent, he ignores a yellowjacket which buzzes about his hard, broad jaw. "I don't bother anybody unless they fuck with me. Then I kill 'em."

A few minutes later, I press him on a question. "Why you fucking with me?" He hollers, grazing a knife in front of my nose.

Born in Bogalusa, Louisiana, Shane spent eighteen months as a medic in Vietnam, then returned to the United States and came to Chicago to live with relatives. "Let's not talk about that," he said; 1983 was the last year he had an address. His bad knee and bad back forced him to walk on crutches; now he uses a cane.

"I don't like nobody," Shane says. "I don't know why I'm talking to you now. Nobody comes around here." Then adds, "How did you find me?" (I told him I stumbled across his house while wandering. Shane howled, "I'm a wanderer," and tossed his head back to close his eyes at the sky.) And actually, Shane was paid a visit once. A member

UNEK

of the toughest street gang in Chicago, the Chicago Police, visited him.

Shane: "This big ol' 6'3" cop came down here, said 'Get the fuck out of here'. I didn't say nothin'. Then he said, 'You better be gone when I come back'. Three months later, in November; he came wearing a snow hat. I was inside [the house], heard my dogs start barking. My dogs was just protecting their territory, they weren't doing nothing wrong. They were only trying to protect me because I saved them from out of the gutter. If you touch me right now, they'll probably try to kill you.

"I was lying on the ground and the cop yelled at my dogs and then shot at one of them with a .38—but I didn't have my glasses then so he might have just fired in the air. Wherever he fired don't matter; the point is, he thinks he can do anything to me because I'm a tramp and I don't have any rights. After that, I had to move away from there to where I am now." Shane left his old residence intact as a decoy to police.

Shane earns enough money recycling aluminum cans and scavenging to sustain a modest lifestyle. Assorted bottles of consumer goods, pots, and miscellaneous household effects are arrayed atop his tarped non-leaking roof, and along exterior shelves of the house which boasts two glass windows and a fireplace. Inside his home, which he calls "the camp," Shane has room enough for a mattress, a small bookshelf which overflows with paperbacks, a cabinet, and a space to spread out his art supplies or invite a guest to spend the night (his comment about not liking anyone was mainly attitude).

Shane's camp may be square in the heart of Chicago, surrounded by the city, but for practical purposes, with dogs to keep him warm in the winter and a mannequin outside to scare away prowlers, he lives as a hermit might live in the backwaters of Louisiana—or Vietnam. He bathes and washes clothes in the river, hanging them out to dry in the air, or over a fire in the winter. He shaves, brushes his teeth, cleans house, and worries about his appearance.

When he's not out scavenging, he spends days reading, listening to oldies on his battery-powered radio, and working on his charcoal drawings, which he refuses to sell. He burns his excrement in a bucket to avoid contamination. (One night he got drunk, poured gasoline all over the bucket, and tried to light it. The bucket exploded in his face and caught him on fire. Luckily, he put himself out. That's how he got his patchy complexion.)   **(1991)**

1994—I went back. Shane's house was freshly burned down. Whodunnit?

THEY DON'T TAKE MASTERCARD
AND THEY DON'T TAKE
AMERICAN EXPRESS

"Your first thoughts?" I once asked a friend who was visiting the frontier for the first time.

"Don't tell anyone about this place; let's live here."

The frontier is the kind of place where you'd expect to stumble on the planet's umbilical cord. If this is God's country, it is God's other country. A braggart from the South Bronx says it reminds him of home. Entire chain-link fences, chunks of building, and telephone poles lay strewn about as in the wake of disaster. Forces of life and death, past and future, seem magnified here, as if great battles had been fought or apocalyptic armies are converging to raise the soil.

But that's all in the imagination. The real ones raising the soil and converging around here are not imaginary armies, but builders hired by developers. Try putting my *What is there to do between China-*

town and Downtown question to John Heimbaugh, developer for the Chinese-American Development Corporation, only one of three groups planning to develop a portion of the frontier. For Heimbaugh, the thing to do between Chinatown and Downtown is clear: build more Chinatown. Heimbaugh hopes to expand Chinatown northward to 18th street, erecting townhouses, condos, a park, a hotel, and a convention center.

If you can believe the architectural drawings which cover the walls of Heimbaugh's office, it is only a matter of years before the Wentworth Avenue ghost city gets lined with fresh asphalt, manicured shrubs, and hordes of goofy shoppers. Someone like me might slice a couple onions, but realistically there's no need to feel nostalgia. As long as the city's population continues to fall, the golden law of urban entropy holds: gentrification in one area insures abandonment elsewhere. If developers keep swallowing up the edges of downtown like this, hell, the next frontier could be State Street Mall.

Out behind the Fame, the river embankment has crumbled away so that it is possible to dangle your feet in the murky water—gray, blue or green, depending on your angle to the bridge, sky or trees— which flushes gently against the roots of overhanging trees.

Downtown, the river seems strangled by walkways and bridges; here, it meanders along, reflecting on its foliage, like a friend taking a breather after a hard day at the office. Here, the river's serenity is disturbed only momentarily by the motorboating yahoos who careen up the river in summertime, heeding only the glory of their own faces in the wind.

Many bridges along the river are equipped with a complex series of steep, sturdy stairways and ladders. Nothing save your own good sense will prevent you from climbing to the top of the 16th Street bridge, where views are dizzying, railings are minimal, they don't take Mastercard and they don't take American Express.

Even some bridge tenders won't climb up there. The bridge's control room is operated around the clock and you have to sneak past it if you want to scale to the top. Once as a friend and I descended from the bridge's heights, we were apprehended by a tender—a thin, curly-haired woman named Rina, who reminds you of someone's mother.

"Keep coming down," she prodded, surprising us as we inched down from a few landings above. "Come on down here. I called the railroad police on you. Come on." My companion and I edged past Rina on the narrow stairway, the threat of police sirening down our spines. "Wait, don't run away, listen to me. Wait, I'll cancel the call to the police." she said. We paused on the stairs. Sensing she had our attention, Rina spoke, stopping every few words for us to consider the gravity of her warning.

"When I lift up this bridge," she began. "Do you realize that the concrete counterweight falls, and the whole bridge structure tips upside-down. Do you think you would survive if I lifted up the bridge while you were on it? When I raise this bridge, I only check to make sure no one's standing on the tracks. I never check up there where you were. Even if you saw a ship coming down the river, do you think you'd have time to climb down?"

There was nothing for us to say.

"Please don't ever go up there again." Rina said.

We thanked her.

"Please, do you realize what it does to me?"

The forest centered around the bridge is almost impenetrable further to the north. I'm positive bodies have been dumped into the river here. Apparently, I'm not the only one who thinks so. Yeah cops, I saw the remains of yo' Dunkin' Donuts conventions. **(1991)**

hip-hop and mental illness
THE TRULY ILLMATIC

A lot of hip-hoppers I know—especially from New York City—act like they are mentally ill. A lot of them probably are. With the rise of adjectives such as "crazy," "sick," "mad," "retarded," "stupid," "ill" and "psychotic," hip-hop can now claim its place alongside heavy metal as the only other subculture to celebrate mental illness.

The first time Nassir showed up at my house at 5 am, ringing my doorbell and waking up my family, I didn't think it was anything strange. There he was, neatly dressed, standing patiently in the morning rain, holding a small garbage bag with clothes and crinkled-up outlines in it.

"What's up man," he would say with an excited grin and I'd forgive him for waking me up. Nassir and I have known each other for eight years. He DJs, raps a little, and at 24, he's one of the few original '80s writers left on the South Side. When I see Nassir, I'm happy just to see him alive.

At the moment, he is living in a men's shelter. Nassir's mind is always on a different plane. He doesn't talk about being homeless. He'd rather talk about philosophy, girls, "You got some cans?" or "Look what I racked from Radio Shack." He is teaching himself Arabic.

Last week, Nassir came over to my house every day for three days straight.

After the first day, my mom said he couldn't come over anymore. She doesn't like anyone in her house, let alone a homeless black man who does graffiti. I explained the situation to Nassir. He said he didn't mind. We could just chill on the stoop and kick some of our wack rhymes.

The third day Nassir came, I wasn't home. Nassir was feeling woozy so he took a nap in the lobby of my building. My neighbors called the police on him.

The fourth day, me and Nassir were back out on the stoop.

My mom came home and told Nassir he needed to find a job.

"Job?" Nassir repeated thoughtfully, "Wasn't he in the Bible?"

I took that as him not wanting to answer the question. I just figured he was creative and smart and weird like every other original hip-hoppers I know.

"Mom," I said. "Quit preaching to people. Nassir would have a job if he wanted one. You don't know anything about him . . ."

My mom ignored me. She was staring intently at Nassir. "You're bringing up things that are irrelevant," she said. "That's a sign of mental illness."

My mom is cold, but she basically has a good heart. She asked Nassir if he wanted her to call his family to ask if he could go back there. Nassir said he would like that.

My mom called Nassir's house and she was right. Nassir's brother-in-law told her Nassir had been diagnosed with mild schizophrenia.

His schizophrenia came on suddenly one summer night in 1987. Nassir and his best friend FUN were surfing on the back of an Evanston train. When the train stopped at South Main station, FUN hopped off the back so he could hit the side of the train with a Magnum. The third rails in Evanston are higher than on the South Side and FUN caught it on his shin. Nassir's last words to FUN were: "Watch out for the third—"

Nassir pulled FUN off the rail, but FUN didn't make it.

Seven years later, Nassir is still trying to put his life back together. He has stopped using drugs. He wants to devote his life to hip-hop and Islam, but no one is really looking out for him anymore.

Nassir is thinking about selling his DJ equipment and moving to New York City so he can "meet up with Rakim and a few other people who will understand" him.

Nassir is not all that hard to understand. He's creative and smart and weird and he's been through a lot of shit—just like every other original hip-hopper I know.

And if the rest of us are going to be out here talking about "Yo, that's crazy, mad, sick, dope, and ill," then we also need to be looking out for the originals among us who truly are.

THE CITY THAT REVIVED BREAKDANCING

In the summer of 1991, Tung Twista, at that time the world's fastest rapper (now it's another Chicago rapper, Rebel XD), wrote a song called Back to School. "Let's go back to school," went the chorus. "Let's go let's go back to school, to the old-school."

No one paid any attention to it. In Chicago, the idea sounded like a restatement of the obvious. A lot of us have never been about anything else. "Chicago, our whole concept of hip-hop comes straight out of *Wild Style*," says Demon. "We swallowed it as a whole package: breakin, rapping, DJing and graffiti together. We never split them apart."

"When things are smaller, there's more of a brotherhood," says Ranks, an NYC writer living in Chicago. "The bigger hip-hop got in New York, it lost that brotherhood. I'd say by '87, it was hard to get respect if you weren't old-school. That's when it started getting a lot more violent. Nowadays, you can't get respect if you don't fight. You get as much fame for hitting someone as you do for bombing. One cross-out is worth 50 tags because people remember your name more.

"Any spot you go to, you gotta bring enough people. People are constantly robbing paint. It used to be racking paint. Now they just wait at spots and rob paint. Every spot is run by a crew. If you don't have a really well-respected name, even if you do have a well-respected name, they'll lie about what they write and then vic you. You rarely see big productions in New York. It's all about getting your name up. You can't sweat anybody. Even if you like their stuff. When you meet them, you have to act like it's nothing. When you meet anyone in New York, you're sizing each other up for a fight."

Chicago in comparison is the capital of hip-hop idealism. People who visit here from other cities are shocked to find how friendly and open we are. "In Chicago, it's still a brotherhood. There isn't a hint of violence in their actions," says Ranks.

"Man, I love Chicago hip-hop," says Giant from Albuquerque. "It's like the closest I've seen to recreating what it must have been like in the early days of New York." Exactly. That's exactly what we're trying to do. That's why the only magazine in the US that gives equal play to DJing, rap, graffiti, and b-boying is *Chicago Rocks*, the monthly organ of the Chi-Rock Nation.

And let no one forget hip-hop's fifth art form: Tinkering—as when Grandmaster Flash rigged up his mixer to synchronize beats: "I was in the experimentation phase of trying to lock the beat together. I had to be able to hear the other turntable before I mixed it over . . . I had to go to the raw parts shop downtown to find me a single pole double throw switch, some crazy glue to glue this part to my mixer, an external amplifier and a headphone. What I did when I had all this soldered together, I jumped for joy—I've got it, I've got it, I've got it!"*

Remember homemade markers, Ang 13 could be heard lecturing shorties at Chi-Rock meetings. "*Remember* the word *homemade*! That's what this is all about." Across the street from me, a grammar-school kid named Lance has been making elastic fat laces. Meanwhile, Cypress Hill gets paid to recycle Rammelzee's old whiny-voiced Beat Bop style from 1983.

Up until 1992, hip-hop in Chicago was like going back in time.

* Quoted in David Toop's *The Rap Attack* London: Pluto Press, 1984.

Rappers here didn't drive cars. (Even Tung Twista didn't have a car, and when he caught the bus people would tease him). Most got more fame from graffiti than from MCing.

"In Chicago, people would ask each other Are you hip-hop? In New York, you don't ask people Are you hip-hop," says P-Lee (DJ Parker Lee), who in the early '80s brought hip-hop DJing and graffiti from Manhattan to Chicago's North Side. "In New York, they don't categorize themselves as hip-hop because people just grow into hip-hop. That's all there was for us. In Chicago, there were two underground musics to choose between. We were a minority fighting that house shit. In New York, there was nothing to fight against."

Hip-hop parties in Chicago were so uncommon that people would go crazy just being there. "When I played 'Scenario', brothers got to jumpin," said Why Not of The Dariens who DJed a party in late 1991. "I looked down from the DJ booth; they were going apeshit. I had to stop the record and calm everybody down so no one would get crushed. In other cities people are mellower at hip-hop parties. They're used to it. In Chicago, we're not used to having this shit, and we go totally crazy."

New school dancers flex impossible noodle-knee steps: Body parts glide around in their sockets, contract, collapse in on themselves, and halt in spellbinding freezes. In the same circle, shoes whirl like blender blades about a single point of contact with the floor: head, back, shoulder, hand, knee, elbow, neckbone, butt—and every other section that, if found on a pig, would probably end up on a plate with mustard greens and cornbread.

After breakin' died in 1986, b-boys here took revenge against house by breakin' in house clubs, which were the only clubs back then. "Breakdancers were like the outcasts," says Faheem. "We tried to tell them it was coming back in. Nobody believed us. They laughed at us. We've been through a lot with this hip-hop." By 1991, it wasn't just the old-schoolers any more. A second wave of breakers was coming up. The new people brought the old people back out. That's when we had the revival.

In March 1992, *The Source* ran an article called "Chicago: The City that Revived Breakdancing." A few months later, *Rappages* picked up the story. By summer, *Urb* was sponsoring old-school roundtables, and The Source ran another story reporting on the old-school revival in the Bay Area. Come autumn, half the world was wearing Adidas, making songs about the old-school, and wondering what happened to Lee, Kool Herc, The New York City Breakers, and The Treacherous Three.

"YOU CAN'T HITCHHIKE TODAY"

And so here it all begins, on the comfort graded chairs of a Greyhound bus headed for Hunter's house in St. Louis. Been reading the wild foods book and trying to memorize the ones I can eat. The grass that grows alongside these highways is terrible. Nothing that resembles food this time of the year that I can see.

I'm feeling kind of bad about this home situation. When I had finished packing, doing mail, and pony-tailing up a few of the many loose ends in my life, I told my father I was going. He knocked on my mother's study door (she had the door closed; usually she prefers to leave it open).

"Barbie, Billy's leaving. Do you want to say good-bye?" my father asked tensely from the doorway. When I entered, my mom was sitting in her chair gazing numbly. With my backpack on, I went over and hugged her from behind in the chair. It was a long hug, and when I let go, she was crying. Her mouth was all contorted like it was filled with horseradish; her eyes were pleading, pitiful. Lately I've taken to ignoring emotions that I can't, or won't, do anything about, but seeing my mom like this kind of got to me. It got me asking myself the why am I doing this question.

My mom's infamous. She hates graffiti. She'd find my phone book and start going down the list calling people at three in the morning. Hello Warp. This is Upski's mother. Do you know where Upski is? You don't know. Well, are you sure? You're sure. Well, do you know if he's out doing graffiti? You don't know. Well who is this Kep person? You don't know. Well is he a rapper or does he do graffiti? You don't know. Well what about Pengo? What's Pengo's real name? You don't know. Is Upski out with Pengo? et cetera.

Any time someone calls my house, she asks if they do graffiti. If they do, she gets upset at them. Her face turns red and she reads to them from an article about the toxic compounds found in spray paint. Certain people are bad-listed. For almost ten years, I have been friends with Raven. He still can't call my house. Three years ago my mom intercepted a letter from him talking about Let's go out bombing. He was *encouraging* me to do graffiti. But mom, he's not a bad influence. He gets straight As. Sure he gets As. *He* wants to make something of himself. He wants *you* to fuck up . . .

Just looked at a weather map of the South. Forecast: bad. Too cold to sleep outside without a sleeping bag which I refuse to carry. I told you about my plan, didn't I? Hitchhiking, freight-hopping, wilderness-surviving, people-meeting, snake-steaking, etc. By mid-spring I should be in New York City or San Francisco. One of those.

I'm hearing for the first time this St. Louis suthen accent. So melodious. Coming into town was heartwarming. In the last stretch, the land grew greener, hillier, more vegetated. No signs of the snow that could be seen forty and fifty miles to the north. It all seemed so unreal, so unimaginable what I was about to do.

I've read all these books in preparation for my trip: one about walking across the country; another about hoboing across the country; another about hitchhiking; another about camping; another about surviving off the wilderness; another about being a traveling news reporter; another about urban exploration and how to climb buildings with your bare hands; another about the new jumbo super-suburbs. It's like damn, they all sound so good, can't I just do them all at once?

A lot of neighborhoods in St. Louis have gates around them. Private fences are illegal. Cats are only allowed out on leashes. Stop signs on every block but no one ever stops at them. Someone from out of town stopped at a stop sign once and was rear-ended. By a police car.

Last night me and Hunter watched these killer movies. In one, a hitchhiker gets shot to death. In another, a camper dude gets fucked in the ass by these psychotic hillbillies. Great preparation for my trip! I usually never let myself watch those type of movies. They're for people who like to sit around their house and get scared of creaky floorboards. This shit is for real. I can't afford to be p-noid.

How many adults have given me the exact same advice in the exact same words? "You can't hitchhike today. It's not like it was in the

'60s." Tryna tell me scary stories, quoting numbers about the geometric rise in serial killers. Whatever you say. The world doesn't seem half as dangerous to me as it does to some people. Even in a place like Chicago, the average person only has about a one in a million chance of getting murdered on any given day (Two and a half murders a day among 2.7 million people). And if you don't hang out with criminal types, your chances are that much better. People have the same irrational fear of snakes. In the US, only about one thousand people get bitten a year by snakes. Only about twelve of them die.

When I awoke on Hunter's couch in St.Louis, I had nothing left to do but mail some packages. It was gorgeous out. I quickly gathered my belongings into my backpack, showered, packed a bag lunch and popped down a pan of cholesterol for breakfast. Hunter wrote this rap called "stick and doo rag rag." Part of it goes like this:

> *I'm gonna hit the road livin life as a vagabond*
> *Dust on my Adidas and the highway's goin on*
> *So I told the world whether or not you like it*
> *I'll be gone for a while, yeah, I'm gonna hitchhike it*
> *So I pack my toothbrush and a Pilot to tag*
> *Settin out on the country with my stick and doo rag*
> *I give that a thumbs-up, It was a red Mercede*
> *The baby pulled over, the driver was a lady.*
> *We talked about the youth, that's when that I told her*
> *I bite the hand that feeds me with a chip on my shoulder*

This is just his indulgent fantasy. Hunter has hitchhiked maybe twice in his whole life. He dropped me off at the post office, and we said the brief good-byes of friends who know each other well enough not to bother with fanfare. I walked to I-55 which goes right past that ridiculous arch, rubberbanded my tear-gas to my right wrist (the side away from the driver), pulled out my "Memphis (please)" sign, and began my as yet short career as a vagabond.

THEY'LL KNIFE YOU IN YOUR SLEEP

After spending that first night freezing under a viaduct in Portageville, Missouri, I learned quickly that hitchhiking was not about eating roadside dandelions and being a loner. Six days, five showers, four houses, eight rides, close to twenty free meals, around five hudred fifty miles driven, fifty miles walked, and hundreds of conversations later, I am well into my lesson of surviving on the road (I have spent less than $4 so far, most of that given to bums in Memphis). Nothing too earth-shattering has happened yet, but every day is filled with dozens of small surprises and clichés of a cross-country adventure.

In Jackson, Mississippi, I was dropped off Friday night around 9 pm in front of this car dealership in the northern suburbs. I began walking along the side of the road in the direction of downtown. I found a main street and I walked for five miles without seeing a single pedestrian. It was the white area of town, a residential area, the cars bursting by like miniature private parties. This town was not meant for me. They didn't even have any sidewalks except for a block here, a block there. I caught one man going into his house from the driveway and made sure I was still going towards downtown. Five or six more miles to go, he said.

A few miles later, I had gotten lost in this out of the way corporate cul-de-sac. I was getting fatigued mentally and beginning to contemplate sleep. Out of nowhere zooms this bright red sports car full of giggling teenage girls.

"Are you lost?" one of them yells out the window.

They come back around for a better look. One of them comes running out to meet me.

"Like, oh my gosh, you're a hitchhiker, that's like, that's so cool."

They tell me to get into the car. I have to meet their friends. They have me sit next to someone's unattended purse. Ah, the pleasures of being white. They drive me to this parking lot where all the private school pop tarts meet each other and drink beer. Forty of them surround me like I'm a flying saucer, shooting me questions with light on their faces. I learn that I am very interesting. I learn that I am okay for a fuckin Yankee from up North. (A few of them begin making self-conscious jokes about "Oh, yeah, we have to go home so we can whoop our slaves.") They fix me up with a beer.

After about ten minutes, they lose interest in me except for a small clique of boys who are worried about where I am going to sleep.

I guess I was gonna sleep downtown, I say.

Downtown? No. They couldn't believe it. He thought he was gon sleep downtown!

Are you crazy?

There's nothing downtown but niggers, one of them points out.

African-Americans, scoffs another. He's from up North.

They'll knife you in your sleep, warns a third.

To prevent this from happening, the boys loan me a sleeping bag and deposit me at the local kiddy park where they are sure I will be safe from knife-wielding African-Americans. They set me up in this big wooden structure and ask me again and again if I am sure I will be okay. I am sure sure sure sure sure. Sure I'm sure. I begin to think they are going to tuck me in. Then they leave and I am alone again.

In the middle of the night, a luxury mini-van slowly pulls up alongside the kiddy park. The door opens and a figure comes running toward me. "Billy. It's Chan." This is one of the boys. "Come on. My father said you could stay with us."

White skin privilege, yo! I'm using it to the fullest.

Chan's family adopted me. Chan's father was a landscape architect, and they lived in an incredible semi-mansion (on "Tyrone Street"). They gave me my own little wing of the house with a bathroom and everything. It was like being an exchange student. It was like being in heaven. The next day I went wandering around Jackson. I was warned not to go to the black side of town because "instant death" awaited me there. So of course I went, and hung out with these thirty little kids who fed me some pickled pig's feet. We played basketball and mattress jumping in the garbage-strewn backyard of this abandoned shack. The gangs are the same as in Chicago: All's Well, VLs, BDs, GDs . . . and everybody down here has relatives in Chicago and knows the names of Chicago streets the way hip-hop fans the world over know Empire Boulevard in Brooklyn or Mott Avenue in the Bronx.

I was asking one of the older kids (about 15 years old) where else in Jackson I should go. She says don't go to Pharis street, that's where the dope dealers hang out at the pool hall and they beat up white people. So I say great, how do I get there? They say no no no no. I say yes

yes yes yes yes. These five kids about 12 years old come with me to "protect" me and we go there and play pool and I meet the drug dealers and then we play for a few more hours on the train tracks and in this creek and then we go to this carnival and stand behind a fence to watch all the white children ride the whirl-i-whirl and the bungee gump. I said it was time for me to go to the library so I could write. None of them knew where the library was, but wanted to go there all the same. So once we get there, they're running around—not quite running—and playing on the two story elevator.

Patronizingly, I caution them to behave, to say "excuse me" and "please" to the librarians, instead of "Hey you," and I suggest that they "read some nice books." This tactic fails, and they decide to call it a day. The last kid to leave, P-shay, asks the librarian for directions to my host's house for me: Excuse me, ma'am, where is Tyrone Street? he asks, shooting me a how-am-I-doing? glance. Twenty seconds later, there is a loud knocking on the window. Everyone looks up from their books. P-Shay waves at me and runs. When the kids give me their addresses, one of the addresses turns out to be in an alley.

I try to scratch down what I see in my notebook, but by the time I write the one thing, ten more things have already happened. I have no goals. Every day is from scratch. Everything tastes delicious, and never have resting or washing been so glorious, but I can never stay in one place for more than a few days because life becomes too easy and then I have to think about what the point of it is. I feel like I'm trying to escape from something.

RIDE FROM A BLACK WOMAN

I have this new philosophy about money. You're going to trip. I got this ride in Daytona Beach from this guy. He was a supervisor for this traveling salesmen company—a pimp of sorts. As a kid he was in and out of jails, group homes, dropped out of school at 16, you know the list. He didn't know how he was going to do it at the time, but he knew that he was going to make money, and then he was going to make *money off of* that money. He got a job at McDonald's, lived at home, and saved every penny. Most 16-year-olds would buy clothes, or go out to eat and party; the best they'd maybe do is save up for a car.

Not my man. He invested his money. A little at a time he bought stocks and found bargains which he resold. At 23, he has half a million dollars. He and his wife live in a big house. He could practically retire now and live off the interest. That's going to be my new strategy too. I already know how to save, now I'm going to learn to invest. Before you know it, I'll be indicted for junk bonds and leveraged buyouts. Naw, I'm buggin. What I really want to do is learn this shit so I can teach it to kids in fucked-up situations. Most people who wish to do good in this world stay away from money. They see what happens to people who have money and they think it's corrupt, unclean. If they go to school at all, it's for English or social work. But if you have the discipline and you know what you want, why not make the money and use it for revolutionary purposes? I am so geeked.

Did I mention before that I'd never gotten a ride from a black person? Maybe half a dozen have given me rides now. One time I even got a ride from a black woman! I was staying in the suburbs of Orlando with this young couple who saw me in the town square making an ass of myself dancing for quarters and took me in (I can't really dance but what did they know!). I had gone down to the library one day, and was trying to hitch a ride home at night. The police rolled up on me and warned me I had to go outside the city limits to hitchhike. I started walking. This girl who had just got off work at 7-11 saw me and asked me where I was tryna go. She said, Oh, you can catch a ride with my mama. Before I knew it we were at her mama's car.

She said, "Mama, give my friend a ride to so-and-so."

Her mama said, "Friend? Where you know him from?"

I must have looked like a killer. I thought it was time to leave.

The girl said, "We went to school together."

I was stunned.

Finally her mom motioned to me, "Well, get in."

Me and the girl tried to make conversation to play it off, but we didn't even know each other's names. It was funny as hell. Her mama must have snapped when they let me out of the car.

With all the men I had propositioning me on that trip—at least one a day—I'm beginning to see how women feel. At 10 pm one night, I was stuck in this place called Oceanside trying to get to LA and nobody would pick me up. I was using the phone when this dude came to use the phone adjacent mine. I asked him if he was going to LA. He said he was, but not until 2 am. I could already tell he was a little bit queer, a black fellow who'd spent a little too much time around white folks. He invited me to come to his friend's apartment with him and wait.

His friend was out of town. Conveniently, he had been given the keys "so we could chill out and relax." We had a lot to talk about. Turned out he was from the Robert Taylor in Chicago. World's biggest housing disaster. I cooked us the world's biggest dinner disaster.

Not that I'm a bad cook. Just that while I was cooking, he was talking to me and he began telling me about how he was bisexual. Okay. It wasn't no thing. I went to Oberlin. Then he started asking all about me. Had I ever tried it? He didn't believe me. Had I ever thought about it? He didn't believe me. And on and on. He just didn't believe me.

He wasn't totally and completely wrong. Homosexuality is a matter of degree and like everyone else, I'm probably at least a little bit bisexual. It's just that my bisexual side is a *very* little bit, and I wasn't about to explore it with him.

At one point, he just said "Sure I can accept if you aren't bisexual. I hope you don't mind if I just sit here and watch . . . the view." Then he proceeded to watch me cook french fries, telling me how fine I was, and how I should really try being bisexual (he didn't think he'd like it at first either). Then he asked if I'd mind posing nude for him. I minded. It ended up he was too tired to go to LA, so he "let" me spend the night on his friend's floor. Then he tried to curl up on the floor next to me, even though he could have slept on the couch or the bed.

It was a long night.

Eventually I got back to Chicago. I left Chicago with $45 in a waterproof pouch. I came home three months later with $30. Yes, I said. Now I can do anything. I don't need money anymore. I can do anything I want and survive and be happy .

That was a lie. My life didn't change very much. Yeah, I saw new places and had new feelings, and learned new things but when I got back home I still had the same old battles to fight. I did what every white boy my age dreams to do but it didn't make me immortal. It didn't make me right or fix my personality or teach me to fall in love. It didn't deliver me from fear, vanity or insecurity. It didn't do any of the things I wanted it to do for me.

133

A Third Wave of Graffiti Sweeps America
STATIONS ON THE NATIONAL SUBWAY

At the moment, there are about fifty graffiti writers in Birmingham, Alabama.

Mare Twoer is a Birmingham native who has been writing since about 1986 when he saw *Style Wars* on PBS. "Rednecks down here were like 'What's this fuckin gang shit?' That's what they think. It's like we were these aliens who come down at night and put this stuff up. They were scratching their heads. How did this get here? Must be those people from up North. They buff our shit real quick. The only one they leave up is TRUST JESUS. They seem to like his stuff. Every time we talk to writers from other cities, they're like: What do you guys paint down there, barns and cattle wagons?"

Bombing didn't really catch on outside New York and Philly until the early '80s. Although imitated everywhere, in only seven major US metro areas did the second wave really take root: Boston, Baltimore, Miami, Chicago, Los Angeles, San Diego, and the San Francisco Bay— along with smaller cities like Portland, Seattle, Pittsburgh and satellites in the New York tri-state area. When the hype over breakdancing settled down, only about a dozen US cities remained noticeably bombed.

By 1994, it's beginning to look more like two or three or four dozen cities along with perhaps *hundreds* of smaller cities and suburbs. The only really major city that still has almost no graffiti is Houston, with Detroit as a distant second. In most cases, local writers were in-spired when big city writers moved to their town. Rasta 68 came to Denver from Queens in 1987. Doc (LA) and Agree (NYC) sparked off Albuquerque in 1989. The same year, LA-based Emer One rejuvenat-ed Minneapolis-St. Paul in collaboration with relocated writers from San Francisco, Brooklyn, Chicago, San Diego, Texas, Columbus, and Madison fucking Wisconsin—which also has about fifty writers

Meanwhile, writers had been hitting freights haphazardly for decades and no one paid them any mind. But as cities wiped their sub-ways clean in the late '80s, graffiti writers ripened for a new outlet, a new challenge. Meanwhile, with the aid of magazines and videos, writers from different cities mingled; the nationwide graffiti scene took form.

With the increasing nationalization of graffiti, freights became the next logical step, says Futura 2000, one of Graffiti's early vision-aries, who in 1986 helped paint the *Detroit Art Train*, a permission piece which was the first multi-car freight burner. "At the time, we didn't take freights seriously," he said. "Now that this is happening, I wish I was ten years younger."

At 38, Futura remembers that New York City's graffiti habit did not start out on subways. It began in, and was initially limited to, cer-tain neighborhoods. And just as it took subways to capture the imag-ination of all New York City, today's freight train pioneers speculate that freights could help export the art in a lasting way to all of Amer-ica—a national subway.

Graffiti's horizons are expanding. "I don't really like the city any-more. It's too violent. Too crowded," says Chicago-based Ages, thumb-ing through *Trains*, a railroad fan magazine. "Aren't these pictures beau-tiful? I want to move out to the Southwest. Montana. Oregon. Alaska."

Cavs, Sent, Sine 5 and Key in New York, along with Braze and Suroc in Philadelphia are credited with being the first to take freights seriously. Now everybody takes them seriously.

"I started going in the freight yards, seeing three and four pieces by people I had never heard of before. That's when I knew it was blow-ing up," says Power, publisher of Hollywood-based *Can Control*, which like most graffiti magazines seems to devote more and more cov-erage to freights with every passing month. By next summer, it may be hard to find a freight train in America that doesn't have graffiti on it.

Nationally, writers are just beginning to study freights: how they are circulated, what critical mass of bombing it takes to achieve nation-wide fame, to what extent freight companies will care enough to buff, how long before graffiti writers everywhere begin to look at freights as a common billboard . . . who's gonna take graffiti king of Oklahoma. "Over the next few years, we should see an expanding knowledge-base about freights," says Futura.

"A lot of stuff I already know," says Zore. "I know when workers have their shifts and when they pull trains out of the lay-up. It's just like everything I heard about the old-school days of New York. We be going in the yards and just partying. As long as you don't write over their serial numbers, they usually won't buff you."

Along with bathroom stalls, freights are one of the few places in America where graffiti is not completely unwelcome. There's already quite a history of hobo graffiti. "My understanding is that conductors do a lot of that," says Ages. "The Mexican guy bending over with the sombrero and pancho. He does it right above the air brakes. That martini glass, it says the pride of Texas. Trust Jesus. Waterbed Lou. Those are some of the uppest people on the lines."

The main thing freight companies worry about is theft and other structural vandalism. "Graffiti is not a system-wide problem," says Jim Sabourin, spokesperson for Burlington Northern. For that matter, neither is hopping: "It would come under trespassing. Certainly we're concerned for safety reasons. Some have been known to be killed, especially in derailment, but it's not a major system-wide problem."

Security and penalties vary from line to line and yard to yard. A lot of yards are starting to get hot. They've pretty much pushed us out of the freight yards," says 2-Quik of Denver.

Most major crews now have branches in other cities, and a growing number of writers travel the countryside, bombing as they go. Wen and Wane from New York are up in viaducts along Rt. 80 through Indiana. Los Angeles graffiti extends hundreds of miles into the desert toward Las Vegas and Calexico. There's a piece on a power plant along Rt. 380 near Greenville, South Carolina, another in a school yard in Chattanooga, Tennessee. "We'd pass through places like Ft. Walton, Florida where it just looks like writers came through, hit, and left," says Scandal.

Where the second wave of cities was introduced to graffiti as part of hip-hop along with b-boying, MCing and DJing, the third wave associates graffiti more with punk rock, techno, gangbanging and skateboarding. "Graffiti became the trendy thing to do in the skateboard community," says Scandal. "Graffiti in all the skating magazines. Boards had graffiti style designs on them. Kids who skated said "I'm gonna tag too." For a while at the mall, every kid with a backpack on would say they were a writer."

If you think of this as the third major wave of graffiti, there aren't many more waves left before every strip mall, town hall, and corporate park in America, the world—maybe even Singapore—is bombed. As graffiti culture becomes universalized, its unity weakens and it splinters off, like rap, into smaller subcategories which have less and less to do with each other.

"No one pieces here except for the select few," says Vez from Albuquerque. "The rest are tag-banger fuckheads. High school kids. They saw that show *48 Hours* on LA tag-bangers and the next week the place was littered with it. They run around dissing stuff and carrying guns. The gang unit does the gangs and the graffiti kids."

As graffiti shifts from an inner-city to an inter-city playing field, the character of graffiti is changing too. "A lot of people say yeah, freights are sucker stuff," says a writer from Connecticut who chose to stay anonymous. "But to get known on freights, you have to seriously bomb. You have to destroy like a million freights. People I trade flicks with in California keep telling me they're seeing my stuff. The suburban kids are really gonna have a chance to do freights because they have cars so they can get to the freight yards. If suburban kids are gonna write graffiti, they should do freights.

"Now it's switching into a whole nother thing that has nothing to do with where it started. Now its like hop in mom's car, *buy* some paint, go down to this *permission* spot, take pictures of it and send them off to graffiti magazines. Graf is switching up because of the suburbs. In the suburbs you have an idea of personal property. In the city, if you bomb a building, the landlord probably lives uptown or somewhere. Up here, if you write on Joe's truck, Joe is gonna flip out and they're gonna have a town meeting about it. Suburbs aren't set-up for bombing. If a kid bombs up here, it'll get out like "Oh yeah, that's Tom Jones. He's Zap 3."

Or Turk. "I had been bombing out here a little bit, just busses, bus shelters and viaducts," says Turk, a new jack from Chicago who moved to Ames, Iowa. "When I went back to Chicago, I was teaching this kid in Elmhurst, Illinois. Yeah, we were bombing the suburbs. He got arrested. His mom went in his room and found my letters and sent them to the graf squad in Chicago and out here. In my letter, I said I was gonna bomb the fuck out of Ames. These detectives from Ames came to my house. I had just moved here. They knew my name,

NEW YORK
JERSEY
PHILLY

Second Generation

Third Generation

everything. They said if graffiti starts showing up in Ames, they're gonna come to my house."

The character of graffiti varies by region. "In Columbus, there are not as many rooftops as in older cities because of the construction of the buildings," says Esa. "There are a lot of neighborhood block watches. They make it hard. But it's easier to rack."

Observes Mare Twoer: The smaller the city, the more you can single out the people doing it, the more you have to stay anonymous. They've had us on local Crimestoppers. They'd give a $1,000 cash reward. A couple people tried to turn us in but they couldn't prove anything. They got their ass kicked.

Emer One from Los Angeles can't stand most of the writers he helped inspire in Minnesota. "They hang out at coffeehouses and go tagging. They like the fruit of hip-hop but they don't like farming. They have no history at all. No foundation. We beat them down and cross them out so that they know what they're doing is wrong. Then they can learn. Toys feel we're being too hard. We tried to parlay for a long time. The only reason we go to that is like a last resort because they're not listening. We're tryna let them know some of hip-hop's invisible ethics and codes. If you go over a piece, your piece has to burn it. We've got this program up here called Graffiti, Inc. It sounds like a good plan, to do murals and get paid. To me, they were an exploitation group set up as an urban front. They caught people and made them sign a contract. They had a camera trying to take pictures of us and ask us our names. Cops coming to their meetings. Graffiti, Inc. has Minnesota sewed up. All these toys are European, coming out of St. Paul. This is the land of toys and tricks. There's tactics to write and not show where you live but these kids just write in circles, may as well point an arrow to their house. That's why these toys are like a disease. All the spots get burnt up. I feel like I'm gonna get snitched out."

The first writers to hit a town influence the direction graffiti takes there (unfortunately many of these "pioneers" from the big city are big time perpetrators: Oh yeah, I wuz in TC5 back in New Yawk. Lee, Dondi, and dem, doze iz my niggaz . . .).

"When someone goes somewhere and bombs a certain way, that's how everyone bombs at first," says Fred One, a New York writer who lives in Chicago by way of Alabama, St. Louis, and Virginia. "My boy Trace in Cincinnati bombs real tall from-the-ground-up skinny letters. When I went to Cincinnati, it tripped me out. That's how other people were bombing too. But as time went on, they started becoming more independent with style."

Where the pioneers of second wave cities like Los Angeles were often lower-class kids, third wave cities were more likely to be sparked by middle-class writers who brought it with them to college. For instance, graffiti in Providence, Rhode Island centers around the Brown and RISD campuses because of student writers from Boston and New York. Washington DC jumped off in 1989 largely because of students from New York, Connecticut, Baltimore, and Philadelphia. Similar patterns are reported in Kansas City, St. Louis, New Orleans, Madison, Columbus, Atlanta, Austin, and Minneapolis-St. Paul.

There is a graffiti message board on the Internet.

On the whole, the '90s wave of writers tends to be older, whiter, wealthier, further removed from the inner city, and less entwined in hip-hop than first or second generation writers.

"Hip-hop . . . I don't know much about the hip-hop scene here," says Exakto who is one of the *more* street-smart writers in the Washington DC area (most of them live in suburban Maryland or Virginia). "The majority of writers in DC are into hardcore or straight-edge (punk rock) music, so they meet up at hardcore shows."

Emer One remembers a time when he barely saw a white writer: "It kind of hurts to see all these Europeans into it," he says. "There were a few back in the day but if you were a square, you couldn't step into the zone. As it spread, that's when the Caucasians got into it. I don't have anything against European writers as long as they're down. At the same time in around '87, as the popularity and money of crack spread, the African and Hispanic populace started to dissipate because they needed to make money slangin."

Even in places like New York, Philadelphia, and Chicago, graffiti has experienced a demographic whitening. The center of graffiti on Chicago's South Side used to be 61st and King Drive. Only one or two white writers ever went over there. Now the centers of graffiti on the South Side are integrated Hyde Park and the Archer avenue Orange Line, where only whites and Mexicans live for blocks in any direction.

But there's no reason to think graffiti will ever be taken over by whites and Latinos. "In DC, the first generation wrote in the city," explains a DC writer who wants to stay anonymous. "The second and third generations were all from the suburbs coming in to go to hardcore shows. Then they started bombing the suburbs too. Last time I went back, it had bounced back to the city again. These kids from inner-city areas have started bombing and have crews."

In the short term (until America is no longer majority white) the focus on freights may contribute to the whitening of graffiti. But that shouldn't stop anyone who wants to do it. Many of the first hobos were black migrant laborers during the early part of the century.

(White women can do it too—my friend Gin and I went to Wyoming and back pretty easily! For black women, I'm not so sure. You'd have to be incredible, like my girl Erica, yeaaa.)

"A brother in a cornfield is gonna get looked at," says Alex Kyle, a rapper who had barely been out of Chicago until two summers ago when me and him stowed away on a freight to New York City for the New Music Seminar. The trip took us two days because we got lost switching trains in Pennsylvania. "I was scared I was gonna get lynched," he said. "But hey, it was fun as hell . . . Where you want to go next summer?"

The next summer, we tried to get to New York again, only we got kicked off the train by rail police in Buffalo and had to hitchhike the rest of the way across the state. We were in a white section of Buffalo and it took us three or four hours to get a ride. And that was before it got out that Michael Jordan's father had been murdered by a salt-and-pepper pair.

When we finally reached New York it was Saturday night and none of our friends were home. They were all out partying. Me and Alex were walking all over Manhattan, tired, dead and dirty, looking for a place to lie down and fall asleep.

I know. We'll sleep in Central Park, I said.

Alex hadn't been to Central Park before. He'd just heard of it. Won't somebody try to kill us? He wanted to know.

Naw, that's all bullshit, I said. I've walked all over Central Park at night. Everybody thinks it's dangerous so nobody goes there. Come on, I said. You pussy.

We finally get to Central Park. All these people are walking around, acting real shady, like. Walking back and forth, mentally ill, playing chess with themselves, going into convulsions. Let's sleep on one of those benches under the light, Alex says.

Are you fucking crazy, I say. That's exactly where we don't want to sleep. You have to sleep in the darkest, most out-of-the-way corner. Someplace that's scary. That's why nobody goes there. So we head for the darkest corner we can find. Hop a fence. Get way into the bushes. Okay, here we are. Here we are. Let's look around. Let's look around. Our eyes adjust to the dark. Our eyes adjust to the dark. We see people. They are getting up and coming toward us. We run out of the bushes. That was a mistake, I say. Let's try some other bushes.

We go try some other bushes and some other bushes and some other bushes. The same thing happens like three times. Every bushes we go, there are people. Now we're desperate for a place to sleep. I'm not going to sleep in this city, Alex says. Let's just keep walking all night and go to sleep in the morning. Then as we're trying to find our way out of Central Park, he sees a baseball field. Enough of your ideas, he says. Now we're going to do one of my ideas. Let's lie down in the middle of that baseball field. We'll sleep back to back—that way we'll at least be able to see if anyone's coming.

Last summer was good. This summer, we're going to try San Diego.

Deep and Ages have also started hopping freights. "It was super slow," said Ages. "It took a lot longer than we thought. We were gonna go to Louisiana but we didn't have enough food to make it. It was super fuckin bumpy and loud and boring. We made it to Kentucky, then we just got bored and came back home."

Ages tells me not to write about freights so that the toys don't mess it up for us. The way I see it, there are thousands of hobos already and a few thousand more isn't gonna be so terrible. Just please be respectful of our little choo-choos. And please please please be careful. Within the last year, a writer from Madison broke his arm jumping off a freight, and Skate CBS from Los Angeles lost his life in a yard.

If you must know more about freights, order Duffy Littlejohn's *Hopping Freight Trains in America* from your local bookstore.

Who said nobody likes graffiti writers? Who said we are urban heroes out here fighting a lonely battle against asinine aldermen, bland walls, and of course, the evil CTA? It ain't true. We graffiti writers are not that noble, and we're not that alone. We are the secret ally of a force much greater than ourselves. That force is the multi-billion dollar auto industry. Every time we fat cap an outside, or even scratch-bomb a window, we've got guys with last names like Ford, Toyota, and Isuzu with us all the way, cheering us on. It's like a team. We go to Washington & State to destroy the subway pillars. They go to Washington DC to destroy the public transportation budget.

That might be encouraging and all, but me personally, I'm tired of doing charity work for General Motors. I don't know if we're gonna have to start a union and go on strike or what, but them motherfucks needs to be paying us. Otherwise, we're helping them fuck up public transportation for free.

And sorry to be getting all personal and shit, but I happen to like public transportation. Cars keep people apart, public transportation brings people together. Cars are the leading cause of drive-by shootings, drunk-driving, pollution, asthma, potbellies, the greenhouse effect, and guess what? car accidents. If cars are inflaming all these problems: violence, pollution, segregation—then part of the solution to these problems is public transportation, the CTA.

ANTCK

CONCLUSIONS

We as graffiti writers need to ask ourselves, do we really want to be against the CTA? Do we really want to help scare away riders? Do we really want to create more reasons for them to raise the fare? As a writer, there is nothing I love better, nowhere in the city I love more, than the CTA. Whether it's climbing on the tracks, playing in the tunnels, or just chillin' in between cars, I think of the CTA as my personal jungle gym. The fact is, we graffiti writers have a very close relationship with the train lines. Yet it is our goal to fuck them up.

If we love trains, then bombing the CTA is biting the hand that feeds us. It does cost money, which takes away from service. It does alienate riders. It does create an atmosphere for violent crimes. Not that I have anything against crime, in fact I've probably done more than my share already, but I do have something against me and my friends growing up with violence when kids from the suburbs don't have to.

Suburbs aren't cute to me anymore. Cities are dying. Suburbs are taking away city jobs, while my homeys are sitting around with no opportunities, building up that anger inside to run out and kill each other. And oh, what a coincidence, suburbanites are the main ones driving the cars.

I don't mean to overgeneralize. I do think cities can get too crowded and expensive and pressurized. And I don't mean to say that all suburbs are the same. Some of them are just as fucked up as the city and some parts of the city are just like like the suburbs. When I talk about suburbs it's mostly as a metaphor for anyone anywhere who makes a problem worse by running away from it. It also happens that a lot of those people live in the suburbs.

They say a problem doesn't get noticed until it reaches the suburbs. You want attention for bombing? You want fame? You want adventure? Bomb the suburbs. (You don't know how to get out there? That's part of the adventure.) Bomb the car dealerships. The farther away and richer, the better: That way they'll know they can't escape from the city they left behind. Who wants to be the one to start a graffiti movement in Schaumburg? Who'll be the king of Orland Park, Hoffman Estates, and Wilmette? Suburban kids have always come into the city to bomb and we've showed them around. It's coming time for them to start showing us around out there.

That's only for tagging. Piecing we can use in the opposite way as tagging. No one ever said we should be piecing the suburbs. Piecing we can use to beautify the train lines. I don't mean hitting the yards where we're still fighting against the CTA. I'm talking about rooftops along the lines. Rooftops are the key to graffiti in Chicago, because they still are, and always have been, the best places to paint illegally and be seen by the most people. There are still hundreds and hundreds of rooftops without good pieces on them. There are hundreds of rooftops with wack, or incomplete, or fading pieces on them. No one in Chicago has yet done a rooftop justice.

Really incredible pieces along the lines might even help attract riders to the CTA. Chicago can become known as the rooftop city. We haven't even begun to paint rooftops in Chicago. Forget painting in hall of fames. Forget punk ass scratch-bombing. Forget walls in the middle of nowhere. That's LA. Forget painting trains that roll once if you're lucky. That's New York. Chicago is an El train city and our medium is rooftops. Chicago is a city of neighborhoods. Our medium is neighborhood murals.

Imagine if the graffiti writers of Chicago all got together and decided to quit bombing the CTA from such and such a date on (especially scratch-bombing). Tell me those TV stations, newspapers, and radio stations wouldn't jump on the dick. The headlines would read: CHICAGO VANDALS PROMISE CLEAN BUSES AND TRAINS. They'd follow us around trying to predict our next move. They'd have to negotiate with us like they do with the gangs.

Otherwise we are just immature little kids who want to express ourselves. We have no power. We have no game plan, no morals, no vision for the future. Otherwise we just follow the example of other cities and we don't invent a damned thing for ourselves. Let them follow our example this time. If we can change our ways for something we believe in, we'll be benefiting the quality of city life, the environment, and our asthmatic fuckin mayor. We'll be showing that we are strong, we are organized, and we are a force to be reckoned with.

Look at it from the police's point of view: if we can change our mind and bomb rich, suburban-type areas instead of trains and buses and poor areas, what else can we do? We have to show that we aren't just a bunch of punks running around with no brains. We have to show that we can organize power. By becoming friends or guardians of the CTA instead of its enemies, and by demonstrating our power in such a public way, we can make graffiti important again. We've been doing the same old shit for a decade already. I'm tired of doing shit I won't be proud to look back on decades from now. I'm ready for something new—ain't you?

SUCKERS DON'T LAST A MINUTE: GOOD RHYME, BAD THEORY

" . . . there is a tragic misconception among whites. They seem to cherish a strange, irrational notion that something in the very flow of time will cure all ills. In truth, time itself is only neutral. Increasingly, I feel that time has been used destructively by people of ill will much more than it has been used constructively by those of good will."

—MARTIN LUTHER KING, JR. *

There's a theory going around which I call the "Suckers don't last a minute theory." According to this theory, "people who are real about hip-hop" will keep doing it, "all the suckers will fall off" and then "we'll know who's real." [†]

This is a nice theory, but stupid. More than a minute has elapsed, and to quote Chuck D (again, out of context), the suckers have authority. Maybe they will fall off eventually after there's no money left in hip-hop, but how many millions of dollars of my stupid hip-hop friends' money do they have to walk off with before their "minute" is up?

And how many of my stupid hip-hop friends will have to constantly choose between their commitment to hip-hop and their commitment to . . . eating, paying bills, taking care of family, and keeping themselves under a roof—preferably of a structure not bearing the words: "mission," "correctional facility," or "THIS SIDE UP"? But *the suckers will fall off.*

Thank you. And when the suckers do fall off, where will all the committed hip-hop artists be then? In the same place as before, except older and with a bottle of wine in their hand.

The hip-hop industry has enough resources to sustain its artists. The problem, like that dude from Pharcyde said: There seems to be something that is messing with the flucture of the money. It's not com-

UNEK

---

* Quoted in *The Playboy Interviews*, Alex Haley; Ballantine Books: New York (1993).
[†] A friend of mine tells me hardcore lesbians have a similar theory . . . Draw the parallels yourself.

ing to me. Damn I'm outta LUCK. Damn I'm feelin SUCK.

That's why we should consider the possibility of becoming a little bit more organized. The point of organizing isn't to exclude anyone arbitrarily or make ourselves into an exclusive, isolationist club ("Fuck mainstream, fuck crossover, fuck Hammer, fuck Onyx, fuck R&B, fuck house, fuck the West Coast, fuck New Jersey, fuck everyone except us").

No, we should welcome all who are willing to hold themselves to a few basic principles like . . . word is bond, pay your dues, show and prove, etc. That way "we" will know what to expect from each other, and "they" won't be able to just come around and mess everything up. But first, there are a couple of little questions that "we" have to clear up:

1. Who exactly are "we" and how does someone become a part, or not a part, of "us"?

2. Why is the group, as we have defined it, the way it is, not wider or narrower?

3. What exactly is our common ground as a group?

4. What exactly is our uncommon ground (which we can agree to put behind us for the purpose of collective action)?

5. What exactly do we want to use our collective power to do?

6. Why is this the best use of our collective power?

7. How can we best use our collective power under the circumstances to accomplish these goals?

Don't skip these steps. Then you'll be all frustrated and surprised when your shit don't work. And don't pretend that *you* won't abuse power too, because you will. *Do* try to do it less than the next guy. Like Bear (from the Zulu Nation Chicago Chapter) says, "If we're going to organize, we're going to have to represent even people who we may not like, and we're going to need checks and balances."

So next time before we get to making demands and holding protests it would be kind of smart for us to first organize our own government structure.

Many people's first reaction to the idea of government is that it would be too confining. "We made hip-hop to escape from and go against society's rules. The only rules we go by are in the heart," we say. "How are we going to put formal, written rules on ourselves? That'll just limit us and keep us from evolving."

Depends on the rules. Some parts of our lives should never have rules, no matter how reasonable. There should never be rules made (and there are too many rules as it is!) regarding style of expression, of dress, of religious belief, ability, or inner-motivation. There should be no rules saying "Stay true," "You gotta have heart," "You gotta have your own style," "You gotta believe in one God." Those things are too personal, too spiritual, and too abstract to make rules about. We should make no laws limiting belief or expression, and we should oppose any laws that have that effect.

We should make rules for the same reason any society makes rules: to help us organize our anger, our expression, our communication, our political power, and our resources a little bit better.

Oops, no, all that paper work, that would just be too boring. Real hip-hoppers are busy expanding their minds with herb and following the Grateful Dead.

An Interview with Super LP Raven

HIP-HOP IS SUPPOSED TO ELIMINATE ITSELF

If Orko is right about the best MCs being graffiti writers, then Super LP Raven has it made. With the possible exception of Rammelzee in the early '80s, I don't know of anyone who has rivaled his brilliance in both rap and graffiti. Going on missions two and three times a week, constantly writing new songs and making straight As at DePaul University, he remains committed most of all to teaching the shorties and living out his vision of hip-hop-based social revolution.

RAVEN: Chicago is the ultimate testing grounds for the future of hip-hop. The way things developed here, we've been alienated by the industry. We're still very different from the national hip-hop community. We still have a chance to re-define it. Gangster rap has taken over the street form of rapping, and we're trying to take it back. In the old days, there was no gangster rap. You were hardcore, down for your crew, down for any battle challenge. The record industry created gangster rap.

We're trying to perfect a lot of the ideals of old-school hip-hop (as we learned them from the media which in itself was commercialized). We see that we don't have to mimic the hip-hop we grew up on. We want to create a cooperative, community-involved form of hip-hop—basically a whole new hip-hop, creatively, politically, racially, socio-economically, using the differences between us—instead of ignoring them—to create an even greater thing.

Look at how the early hip-hoppers in New York were dressed all bummy and out of style, fat shoe laces. People think rappers are supposed to be cool. I used to be a geek. I would go to school with my nappy fro, thick glasses, and my homemade daishiki.

["Yeah," interjects Lunch Box Law. "When I first met Raven I wanted to be a thug. Me and my thugs, we used to call him names in music class—NERD! We're still one of the nerdier crews in the city."]

In New York, some hip-hoppers concentrate on the history so much they think they're at the end of it already. It's a superiority complex. In Chicago we have an inferiority complex. There are good things and bad things about each one. They're faster to get cynical. We're stuck thinking we're wack. No matter how dope we are, we'll always look down on ourselves. But the advantage is you're always the underdog. That's what's so beautiful about little towns. They're wack. Even when they get good, they still think they're wack. Lunch Box always says people learn from pain. People who've been hurt the most involuntarily become the most intellectual.

Tell me about these pieces you're doing

A few months ago, I realized I can turn anything in the world into a style. I could make a style out of this belt buckle. I could make a style out of a plant. I could make a style out of a cloud. I could make a style out of the inside out of a rusted out spray can with spiders and worms crawling out of it . . . I was telling this to Zore. I picked up a bottle cap. I said, I can turn this into a style. You turn it so the soft side is facing you. Then you put a spiral cut into a cone. Like a drill bit. Then put steel balls rolling down the spiral. Then give it wings . . . here, I'll draw it for you. But then Zore came up to me. He said, you know artists are really liars. Remember, that bottle cap is really somebody else's style. Reminding me of the ultimate foundations of everything. That bottle cap, maybe it was inspired by a plant that was shaped like that.

Zore taught me that all graffiti is based off the tag. That's your base. If you can do a wildstyle tag, make it thick. You can do wildstyle. These are common sense things. I do my pieces without sketches on the wall. I memorize my rhymes. Same thing with the pieces. I make up a style and then I draw it over and over until it becomes discipline. I want to make it so you can reach into the piece. I want you to be able to climb through my pieces, drive on my pieces, get lost in my pieces.

Yes, I love that idea so much. People have always stuck outside objects into their pieces, like sampling a record, they'd sample a picture of something into their piece. But that wasn't evolving the style. It could still stagnate. Now you're saying graffiti is just as limitless as any other art form. I was thinking about, you know, the way a rapper will freestyle about anything around them. What about a graffiti writer who can go up to a wall and look at a tree or a broken-down car or a landscape that's right there and invent a style that's based off that thing. Then a person walking by would see the thing and the painting playing off of each other. That would rock my fuckin world.

Right now the main problem is most of these styles I've done on permission walls. If these styles were on trains or rooftops, they would change Chicago. I'm not just trying to make wildstyle between letters, but to allow each letter to manifest its own inner-style. I'm working slow on it because I want to make wildstyle connections between these wildstyle individual letters which really make that shit an explosion on the wall.

My style is mathematical. Zore taught me about how graffiti was mathematically constructed. I said Damn, that's just like my rhymes. It's about proportion, balance, syllabic distribution. I try to create a beat within the words of my rhymes. Right now, my graffiti is still two-dimensional. The message you communicate is another dimension. The feeling you communicate is another dimension. Is the piece happy or sad? Can you make a style that feels like drinking lemonade on a hot day?

RAVEN

149

RAVEN

I'm still a novice when it comes to style. Every time I'm beginning to think I'm dope, a motherfucker pulls the rug out from under me. I went to Ohio to visit my homey Geeklove. On the wall is this bad ass piece. It's basic New York style, but it's so fresh. It had these little goblets of color that just had color pouring out of them. I stood there looking at it for like 25 minutes, studying it, loving it. And I knew from then that I was wack, not to be so confident.

I learned from overconfident writers that I gots to keep myself in check. Most old and new schoolers are drowning in false self-confidence. So instead of wrestling with ourselves and our own inadequacies, some writers find it easier to find fault with the rest of the graffiti community. If we would all simply fulfill that ultimate role model hardcore writer ourselves, there would be no need to complain.

Like Ages said, if you aren't making up your own style, you're working in gobbledy-gook. You don't have any footing. As soon as somebody makes you aware of where your style came from, you're lost. New York writers can trace their historical growth. They know where that arrow, that connection came from. I don't have that historical grounding. The ground could fall from under me at any time.

That's what I admire about Ages. He spent the time to go beyond Chicago and study graffiti in other cities. He asks questions of as many people as possible, and he listens. That's how you get an understanding of who you are and of what the style you're doing is made of.

Does it seem like people have given up on reading wildstyle?
I was thinking about it, people never did read wildstyle in Chicago. That's 'cause only a few people in Chicago did wildstyle. Every piece from the old school I could read. It should be, after you study someone's wildstyle once, you should be able to read anything they do in that style—if the style makes sense. Study the wackness too, and how you would have done it differently.

When is graffiti gonna change something besides just a wall? Writers will tell me to shut the fuck up on that one. People say it's all about fame, but fame requires community. So if we've got a community, what are we gonna do with it? Usually the ones who are the least dope are the ones who have to advertise it. Hip-hoppers are desperate people. A lot of us are lost. That's why we seek out cultures to express ourselves.

I used to piece and rhyme positivity. That was when De La came out. They tricked me. I tricked myself because I thought they were rhyming on the some positivity, but really they were the ultimate egotists. "Me, Myself and I." The ultimate cocoon. Fuck the community.

I was influenced by a lot of people . . . I'll never forget MC Breeze, the singin MC. Discombobulator Boobulator—yeah boy. And the man who changed all of our lives, KRS-ONE. The Teacher. I started re-listening to KRS-ONE in 1991 and I was with a woman who wasn't interested in rap. She said she'd heard it all before. At first I said you're an outsider, you don't understand. But she was right. Sometimes it takes an outsider to see clearly what's going on. With KRS-ONE, even from the beginning I felt that he was taking the place of the kings he was criticizing. The real thing for me was to be a student, a learner, rather than an overrated teacher.

What are the barriers your'e running up against?
We get stuck in the statement of problems. Hip Hop is a process which is supposed to eliminate itself. For hip-hop to achieve its goals it would have to disappear. Wack public schools breed hip-hop. If hip-hop is going to do something about wack public schools, and it works, then hip-hop will become obsolete, a thing of the past. That's why

hip-hop keeps coming back, 'cause the problems are still there. The industry knows this. That's why they try to continue it as much as possible because they make their money off the problems they perpetuate. It's scary to think you could get rid of hip-hop, but that's the dope part too. Because you're replacing it with something better, and it means you've gotten rid of the wack shit too.

There are a lot of solutions. Look at the Chi-Rock Charter, but we have to be more creative. Until now, hip-hoppers have shielded ourselves from the greater social context. We have to see the similarities between ourselves and those outside of us, and we have to admit to the differences within us. I want to find more ways to involve the community with hip-hop, and to involve hip-hop with the community, with the kids, and with community organizations that already exist. We need to own our own land. There are already people out there who've done what we're trying to do. Hook up with the punk rockers. Hook up with the people who rehabilitate housing for poor people. We learned the shit from *Beat Street*. If you can get electricity to do a party, you can get electricity to live.

So what is it you're exactly trying to do?
I want to redefine what competitiveness means because the way we battle at present is self-destructive. I want to redefine what beef means. Redefine the educational system away from this authoritarian, selfish, rigid, egotistical thing, to create systems where the teacher is a learner too, where the teacher stays active in the art and he's got the test just like new jacks.

The good thing about rap in Chicago remaining underground is that it didn't split off as much from breakdancing and graffiti. Chicago was the prime place for what we're doing to happen. Rap has divorced itself from hip-hop. We're trying to piece our culture back together. Geeklove, he wants to be a renaissance man. Riot from Ill-State already is a renaissance man. He can do all the elements: break, rhyme, DJ and write and he's satisfactory at everything. And ol boy can beatbox too.

Recently we've limited our communication to the open-mic commercial stage. It seems like Chi-Rock is the only place left where I don't have to pay to see my homeys rap. We have to recognize that there are 1,000 different voices in hip-hop. We have to find where they sing in chorus, and to isolate our differences—because you have to recognize your differences before you can unify—then we can unify on the few similarities that we actually have.

RAVEN

For the most part, hip-hop is multicultural. It really is. But there's all sorts of power relationships in it. The most powerful is old school/new school. The fresh and the wack. Men and women. Different races. Rich and poor. There's a myth that we're a multicultural art form that accepts anyone.

That's a goal! When white people started moving back into South Shore . . .Man, black people are beautiful. This was like the perfect opportunity for revenge, dammit. But people just accepted them as part of the community. That's how hip-hop is too. As a black person, it makes me so angry sometimes to see how fucked-up the world is and to see these people benefiting from it.

So how do you deal with that when it's in hip-hop?

One view is that a rich white hip-hopper has to prove himself more. I think the truth is that they can get away with more, just like I got away with more because I was a nerd. One person I know says you have to go to jail. That's when you really lose some of your privilege. There are white political prisoners. They are more a brother than any of us on the outside could ever be. Think about it. Some white motherfucker tries to gank his company to get money for different liberation organizations. I guarantee you'll get respect from the brothers in jail.

Brown brothers really, because half the time a Mexican or a

Puerto Rican is just as fucked up as the black motherfucker who's talking. A Mexican will say, "You don't know shit. Fuck you." We have to be together to have strength against the white superiority complex. I hang with all sorts of hip-hoppers. More brown than white, but all the white are super down. That's like the perfect ratio. You gotta remember, that's how it was since its conception. There are a lot of poor white kids with single mothers on welfare who're into hip-hop.

And you have to remember, a lot of us black boys that went to places like Kenwood didn't fit in in the hood. I lived in the hood, but my family was insulated. I was one of the only ones who seemed like they had a whole family. I heard a lot of gunshots but I wasn't there. My parents made sure I was in by nightfall. Most of those who are in college, except some of the athletes, were insulated. Our parents protected our asses.

My parents ingrained in me Afrocentric views on life. They sent me to IPE [Institute for Positive Education]. IPE taught me it was good to be me, good to be a black person, and with the group of kids I was with. A lot of black kids don't know that they can be them. The confidence is sapped from them and it's replaced with a suicidal hopelessness. Just read Kunjufu. I could give you a list of ten books that show things are set up against brown children to learn.

In my relationship with Risha, we always have to be aware of the power relationships between us. I dominate over her as a man, and she dominates over me as a white and economically. What I decided is that this should be made into a benefit for as many people as possible. We hold each other responsible. If Rish is going to be a doctor working in poor brown communities, she gains from my experience. I make her pay attention to the privilege that she has. From her I have gained insight into my responsibility to the world. Rish and KRS-ONE are my greatest influences. She says: You're a dope rhymer, don't waste time on the mic with that egotistical shit. I still got battle rhymes for the suckers, though.

I've been involving myself in Chi-Rock, working one-on-one with new writers and rappers, working with the young cats. We're doing hip-hop, not as an individualized thing which separates you from the community, but which welcomes them. Almost every piece I've done lately has been meaningful and community-based. It becomes more powerful because people can relate to it; it's involved, not separated.

I'm planning to start-up a reading group for writers and rappers. To have all of us read the same book in a month and do pieces and write raps responding to it. Or we could all watch . . .. *Beat Street* and talk about how it shaped the way we see hip-hop. Okay, it pitted Ramo and Spit against each other without showing the larger forces that both are facing, and had them battle to the death. We all walked away from that movie hating Spit. I was like yeah, fuck Spit. He was probably just a poor, lonely motherfucker with no confidence.

We have to ask ourselves whether we have taken on the attitudes from the *Beat Street* mentality. Whether we are emulating the world around us or whether we are changing it, 'cause that's what hip-hop is supposed to be about. Like Chuck D at the Art Institute kept saying, black people need to take control of the industry—which is true, but a lot of times when we do, we end up doing the same things that the white corporations are doing. It's the eternal struggle of how to fight against a problem without becoming it.

MINISTER FARRAKHAN,
MEET THE BEASTIE BOYS

[okay, both of you can go now]

A lot of people take one look at the lifestyle of someone like me: the dropping out of college, hitchhiking, graffiti writing, and suddenly it all clicks for them: "He's a modern day beatnik / Easy Rider / Huckleberry-Knuckleberry Finn, a rebel in search of freedom from the restrictiveness and hypocrisy of society."

The beatniks, and their modern day corporate counterparts, the Beastie Boys, ran away from society by getting into chemicals and the thrill of the moment. Easy Rider ran away on a motorcycle. Huck Finn, well, he just ran away. I am not running away. I am only running around. My adventure is to be more, not less, involved in society. I left college to become more, not less, educated. I do graffiti to communicate with people, not to push them away.

Chemicals hold no interest for me, I'm scared of motorcycles, and most of the time I'm too caught up in the big picture to lose myself in the moment. As for the whole anarchist fuck-society routine, I don't find it impressive. It's usually either an insincere pose or a naive copout. Sometimes it is a very sick eccentricity. Most of the time, it is people who sit around, smoke bud, complain, and build thin fantasies for themselves around books like this one (or songs or raps) written by defiantly half-baked juveniles with egos the size of America.

GTEK

Opposite the crazedly individualistic Beastie Boy is the Nation Man, the member of a group, the self-sacrificer: the Five Percenter, the gang member, the revolutionary, the follower of Farrakhan, the socialist, the sub-culturist, the afrocentrist, the activist.

Both the Beastie Boy and the Nation Man dislike ordinary society and feel themselves separated from ordinary people—THE IGNORANT MASSES in their minds, who need only to WAKE UP and see the LIGHT. But where the beatnik escapes into art, sex, chemicals, and the open road, the Nation Man escapes into the group with a larger-than-life mission.

"There is a fundamental difference between the appeal of a mass movement and the appeal of a practical organization," writes Eric Hoffer in his classic book *The True Believer* (1951). "The practical organization offers opportunities for self-advancement, and its appeal is mainly to self-interest. A mass movement attracts and holds a following not because it can satisfy the desire for self-advancement, but because it can satisfy the passion for self-renunciation. The innermost craving is for a new life—a rebirth. Faith in a holy cause is to a considerable extent a substitute for the lost faith in ourselves."

While joining a nation or a cause is for many people an enlightening first step into the world of self-discipline, confidence, and powerful ideas, it should only be the first step. Thinking too much as a member of any group or movement tends to make you narrow, two-dimensional, dull, and prejudiced.

What I genuinely find attractive is neither the cowboy individualism of The Beastie Boys nor the organizational unity of The Nation of Islam. It is the synthesis of both. Suppose we could weave together the personal freedom of the Beastie Boys with the personal discipline of the Nation of Islam. The creativity and fun of the Beastie Boys with the character and commitment of the Nation of Islam.

The capitalism of the Beastie Boys with the collectiveness of the Nation of Islam. The iconoclasm of the Beastie Boys with the reverence of the Nation of Islam.

And suppose we could leave out the Beastie Boys' irresponsibility and the Nation of Islam's self-righteousness. I think there are a lot of people who would be down for a movement based around the meeting of those extremes. People who could swing with either side if they wanted to, but are looking for something a little more sensible, a little more universal, a little more practical and down-to-earth.

IN SEARCH OF HIP-HOP'S MORAL CENTER

There's a lot of mixed messages and contradictions in this book. That's intentional. It may seem like a weakness but it's not. Hip-hop's moral center isn't a magical truth out there waiting to be discovered and clutched tightly. It is the understanding that there are many kinds of truth, none of them magic, and all of them competing with each other in the real world.

The best solution is not to choose among the truths, but to juggle them. The great mistake of politics throughout history has been to unite people by dividing them from other people. The juggler seeks out and brings out the good side in all people, be it warring crews; toys or masters; Folks or Brothers; Bloods or Crips; criminals or the police; pro-life or pro-choice, liberals or conservatives; so-called revolutionaries or the so-called government.

The juggler may dis someone, but there has to be an underlying respect. As Kool Moe Dee once said, "Consider rapping as a competitive sport / And we're all enemies on the court / But when the game is over I'll shake your hand / Give you a pound 'cause you're still my man."

The juggler is free to be more radical than the radicals, more conservative than the conservatives, and more moderate than the moderates. Like a hip-hop DJ or producer, jugglers sample the best parts from everything to make for themselves a new track—musically, morally, culturally, spiritually, politically, and economically.

Instead of saying "Fuck society, this is hip-hop," The juggler takes a more sophisticated outlook: "Fuck certain aspects of the way society is now, fuck certain aspects of the way hip-hop is now, and fuck certain aspects of the way I am now."

As LL Cool J says: There's no category. For this story. It will rock in any territory.

As a student of hip-hop, the juggler respects the pioneers, but does not romanticize them. The pioneers were inventing hip-hop as they went along, and soon they had lost control of it. Informal values were attached, but there wasn't the luxury to sit down and specify what those values were. The loosely defined values were good for a time when hip-hop's arena was the playground and the train yard. Today hip-hop is the world's predominant youth culture.

A generation of kids now looks to hip-hop not only for art and entertainment, but for guidance and moral leadership. Hip-hop has been unable to provide that leadership because hip-hop itself prescribes no moral vision.

Too easily, the original meaning is separated from the style, then the style itself becomes the focus. The style means all things to all people; it is anyone's bitch, a medium for good as well as evil, greatness as well as garbage, for or against its original intent. For or against the spirit . . .

Of competition as opposed to bloodshed.

Of using many different histories of music to form a single groove.

Of a groove put together by hands of those at the bottom of society.

Of simple enjoyment through art, social life, adventure, challenge, and self-discipline.

Of living as you believe, whether or not it is socially acceptable.

Of creatively converting insults (such as bad meaning bad into bad meaning good).

Of what you do and the kind of person you are, not who you know, money, status, or looks.

Of sharing and generosity.

Of overcoming isolation and broken homes by creating family out of friends.

Of going all-city, all-world, not being confined to your neighborhood or upbringing.

Something too cooperative and underdog-based to align itself with the American system of elitist republican capitalism.

Too individualistic and materialistic to align itself with socialism or communism.

Too orderly and traditional to align itself with anarchy.

Too diverse and technologically sophisticated to fall off into tribalism.

Too religiously diverse, and too scientifically based to align itself with any one religion.

Too mongrelized and multi-racial to align itself with any one race.

Too rooted in lower-class New York City black and Caribbean experience for others to gain a place in it without having to change their whole lifestyle and outlook.

Too broad, universal, and welcoming to align itself wholesale with anything.

The spirit is still there. It used to be called hip-hop. I don't know what it's called anymore, but whatever it is, it needs to be the new blueprint not only for hip-hop, but for the future of America, suburbs and all.

RAVEN

WHY THIS BOOK IS SO DOPE

Because of the people who worked on and contributed to it: Marc Spiegler, Matt Stephens, Victor Savolainen, Harrison Williams, Desie, Rory Lampert, Nikole Cook, Erica Thornton, Slang, Deep, Antck, Unek, Gin Kilgore, Josh Mason, JP Chill, Jessica Branson, Ahmir Hampton, Nerd, Morgan Pruitt, Gtek, Super LP Raven and Geek of Stony Island, Kanya Freidrich, Jim McNeill, Rob Benavides, Reginald Jolley, Kwame Amoaku, Ken Hollis, Margarita Garcia, Kati Punnett, Rich Gage, Illinois Arts Council, Mom and Dadski.

And the people who mentored me in hip-hop: Bryant Parks, Iggy, Kase, Salahdin, Verse, Fantum, Caution, Warp, K-Lite, Geoffrey Watts.

The people who stuck their neck out to help me write and be read: Wayne Brasler, Steven Gilbert and Darlene McCampbell from high school. Jon Shecter and Ronin Ro at *The Source*; Alison True, Michael Lenehan, and Holly Greenhagen at *The Chicago Reader*, Greg Kot at *The Chicago Tribune*; Sheena Lester and Randolph Heard at *Rappages*; Sacha Jenkins of Ego Trip; Haji Akhigbad of *Beatdown*; Andrew Patner; Rob Kenner and Emil Wilbekin at *Vibe*; Bill Boisvert, Josh Mason, and Matt Roth of *Grey City Journal*; David

Moberg at In These Times; Calvin Hernton, Carol Tufts, Diane Vreuls, Stuart Freibert at Oberlin College; Ben Kim at *New City*, Mark Surface and Ari of On the Go, B-Boy B of *Fly Paper*, D. Artistic Roberts of *Chicago Rocks*; Max Gordon at the New Press; Bill Scher and Jennifer Aronson of *The Oberlin Forum*, Carla Cole and Sarah Van Gelder of *In Context*, Scoop Jackson of *The Agenda*, Ken Kurson at Harper's. Tom Frank at The Baffler. Josh Levine at *Urb*. Pat Collander at *Illinois Times*, Charles Edwards of *Each One Reach One*, Susan Herr, Adolfo Mendez, and Dennis Sykes at *New Expression*, Jake Austen at Rocktober, Noel Ignatiev, Kingsley Clarke, and Hal Adams at Race Traitor, Ed and Dave at *Lumpen*, Answer: Aerosoul.

My influence and inspiration: Phase 2, Sane, Lee, Freedom, Wynton Marsalis, Maya Angelou, Nelson George, Steve Bogira, Saul Alinsky, KRS-ONE, De La Soul, Bill Stephney, Ronald Kahn, Abdul Alkalimat, Daniel Radosh, Melissa Fay Greene, Duro Wicks, James Baldwin, K-Ill, Ice Cube, Kwame, James Bernard, Large Professor, Crazy Legs, MC Breeze, Zore, Alex Haley, Rakim, Wes Jackson, Del, MC Lyte, Cashus D, Common Sense, The Pharcyde, Afrika Bambaataa, Kool Moe Dee, Eldridge Cleaver, Jacob Holt, Chuck D, Mike Royko, Ralph Nader, R. Kelly, Trust Jesus, Karen Rechtschaffen, Robert Krulwich, Ira Glass, Mom, Dad and Nonny.

For friendship flat out: Kie, Hunter, Matt, Rene, Rhea, Marguerite, Ben, Maiko, Kevin, Skye, Danny, Gin, Brian, Cush, Steven, Lesley, Erica, Fere, Wyatt, Beloved, Marc, Mario, Artistic, Lavie, Kanya, Desie, Alex, Ang 13, Thomas, Risha, Rebecca, Nikole, William and Sarajo, Sheira, Sabrina . . . I love y'all.

Because of the Chicago originals who are still out here rocking: P-Lee (DJ Parker Lee), Stane (Akbar), JMD, Black AG, Quicksilver Cooley, Melody, E-Ski, Rob, Trixter, Tronix, Popcorn, Slang, Kingdom Rock, Chainsaw, Cash, Trax and K-Tone, Pac Man, Faheem, Prodigy, Toxic, DJ Shawn, Khalif, Rahiem, Scope, Speedy, Rafa, Nightmare, Fanon, Stereo, Hangman, Triple, Denz, Sinister Def, Cavalier (Tung Twista), Vakil, DA Smart, MC Cat, Connect Flow, Nalej, Pengo, Ice Cee, Comet, Spike 153, Taco Bops, MC Fresh and Wild, B-boy B, Kay-Rock, Kool Rock Steady,

Ease (Jesse Dela Pena), Heckle, Kapri, Kero, Tumchee, Chosen, Awesome A, Rhyme Poets, Defski, Hollywood and Casanova, Donald D, Dean Four, Aztec, Shaggy, Stream, Aaron Brown (Crunch), Kaos, Relic, Taygo, D-Agony, Venom, Kato, Prove, Ray, Tsel, Puma K, Tommyboyskee, The Molemen, Orko, LSD, Poet, EQ, EC, Ages, Snake Roc (The Strangler), Lunch Box, Clarence, Red, Disrok, Casper, Easy Reese, Trust (Love), Telly and Flee, Rebel XD and DJ E, Mack, Titan, Shockwave, Severe, Drastic, Kep, Ah-J, East, Rooster, Swipe Dog, Net, LCD, Tray Mack, Riot, OZ, Crush . . .all the people I don't know about. And all these quik-to-learn new schools keeping everything fresh.

Assorted reasons: Libby at Garfield Press, Psalm, Eric Kozak, Bear, Scribe, Jeckle, Gordo, Enoz, Pilot, Preach, Fun, Kre-8, Hate, Reveal, Kiner, Same, Power and Charlie of *Can Control*, Chris Babbington, Tarek Thorns, Chris Jenkins, Kierna Mayo, Twice, Geneva Smitherman, Dino, Juice, GQ, Jennifer Lister, Carol and Kenny, O-Type Star, Byam Alexander, Ewok, Paul Teruel, Dan Brudney, Dan Charnas, Larry Mondragon, Chris Wilder, Wendy Day, Luis, Fuego, Alan, Junebug, Coqui, Sip, Dolly, Drip, Rome, Doug Mitchell, Nana Yaw Ampofo, Anthony, Donna, Akwanza Gleaves, Charlie and Carl Gibbons-Kilgore, Imani and Malik Wornum, Raymond and Mic, Kelli Curry, Exakto, Chris Coelho, Nanette Vinson, Esa, Chi-Rock, Zulu, Gesa Jager, Cait Kinahan, Prove and Hens, T La Rock, Rory's Mom, Bill and Adele, Ramelle and Ari, Foul, Jamarra, Soke, Osco, and Ku-laid, Fred One and Steph, Alicia Bassuk, Henry Hardee, Jamie Miller, Whatever his name is (What's his name?), Tonae, Amel, Greg and Bobby Sox, Bill West, Alex Alleruzzo, First Lady, The Rosmans, Nonya, Michael Lacoque, Karen Gill, Emanuel Basley, Martay the Hip-hop Wiz, Jellow, J-Bird, Cherie, Matt, Sis, and Tricie, Lindsey Maxwell, Dave Dred, D-Zine, Ed Young, Cheba, Amy Rosenblum, Sol, Ack, Carla Solomon, Clarence III, Charles Edwards, Zia, Grafik, Teal, HS, Slope, Jay Mulberry, Corey Olds, Drastic, Jennifer Zinn, Mary Datcher, Salim Muwakkil, Chet, Foe, Pete Miser, Theme and Shareef, Amy Hundley, Tawa Jogunasimi, Giant, Demon, Patty Stern, Bill Finley, Kirk, Nico, Precious, Oak, Sharon Thornton, Leslee Snyder, Randy Young Dr.Wax, Shake and Terry, Max, Trickey, Billy, Mareika, Audrey, Gnee, Rhonda Dobbins, Tina Howell, The Bransons, Scandal, Emer, Cycle, Hush, Diane Black,

Kuaze, Calvin Baker, Braze, Dream, Turk, Rae, Floyd, William, Granja and Sons, Mara Esposito, Thor, Elizabeth Dwyer, Mary Hynes-Berry, Tomika, Rishi, State of Mind, Jim, Joe Williams, Ben Hall, Gar, Bkuz, Venom, Marianne Potje, Stacy, Leggo, Eddie, Danielle, Coke, MK, Cue, Enski, Hers, Egypt, Mercedeez, Derrick, Bryan, Maureen, Erica, Shockwave, Awesome, Dominic, Michael Warr, Meeshell, Dan Kiss, Sprite, Mane, Bize, Smerz, Tree, Maya, Mark Armstrong, Prashant, Eric Deback, Mike Ilic, Mike Treese, David Meyer, Scott, Yehoshua Peterson, Daria, Seven, all the independent book and record stores who carry our book, and everyone who picked me up along the highways.

Bomb the Suburbs isn't just a book. It's also a plan. The plan is to build an institution that will do on a bigger scale everything we talk about in the book. For starters, we need a Bomb The Suburbs Building For The B-boy Homeless, a studio, computer lab, library, party space, a kitchen, a printing press, and abandoned lots for gardens.

Then we can publish and distribute other original books and albums at cheap prices; bring stability, and creative alternatives to the city; serve as a national center for the advancement of young people and the destruction of ghettos and suburbs; and keep a couple dozen of our friends from falling off the edge.

If you like the book, let us know how you want to become part of the plan.

INDEX

Abused phrases, 7-9
Africa, manhood and
    womanhood in, 91-92
Africa's Gift to America
    (Rogers), 90
Afrikan art, European
    vs., 91
Afrikan culture, aliveness
    of, 90-91
Afrikan values, in rap
    music, 89
Ages (graffiti writer),
    135, 142, 151
Agree, 135
Akinyele, 16
Ali, Muhammad, 29
Allen, Harry, 79, 101
"All good", 8
"All that", 8
*All You Need to Know
    about the Music
    Business* (Passman),
    99
Anarchism, 156
Ang 13, 124
Ant Banks, 14
Ari (graffiti writer), 114-
    15
Armah, Ayi Kwei, 90
Arrested Development,
    18, 87
Art
    European vs. Afrikan,
        91
    graffiti and, 14
Artistic (writer), 77

Atlantic Monthly, 79
*Autobiography of
    Malcolm X, The,* 60,
    96

Baldwin, James, 41
Bama UGA, 84
Bambaataa, Afrika, 19,
    93, 96
Bass, 14
B-Boy B, 73
Beastie Boys, 24, 156-57
Beatdown, 70
Beatniks, 156
Bernard, James, 77, 78
Big Daddy Kane, 14, 24,
    66
Billboard, 73
Biz Markie, 14, 16
Black History Month, 90
Blacks
    acceptance of whites,
        39-40
    anti-white sentiment
        among, 37-39
    basis of white attitudes
        toward, 30-31
    defensive behavior, 37-
        38
    lack of control over des
        tiny, 87
    rap and community
        change, 92-93
    response to criticism,
        34-35
    social condition of, 89-
        90
    whites' fascination with,

31-33
Black Sheep, 67
"Black Steel in the Hour of Chaos", 89
Blackstone Rangers, 84
Blues, 87
"Blunt", 7
Bobbito, 79
Books, Nation of Islam's teachings, 20-21
Brand Nubian, 14
Brat, The, 70
Braun, Carol Moseley, 29
Breakdancing, 17-18
  Chicago revival, 123-26
Breed, 13
Brooks, Gwendolyn, 29
Brown, Aaron, 85
  interview with, 86-93
Brown, James, 87
Burrell Advertising family, 29
Busta Rhymes, 14
Butts, Calvin, 101

Can Control, 70, 135
Cash Money Marvelous, 18
Cashus D, 92, 93, 19
Central Park (New York), 141-42
Chan, 130
Chicago
  description of, 102-6
  graffiti Wall of Fame, 107-9
  hip-hop journalism, 70

hip-hop parties, 125
hip-hop revival, 123-26
homelessness, 117-19
neighborhoods, 29-30
rap and hip-hop separation in, 152-53
rap in, 16-17
real estate development, 119-20
river bridges, 120-21
as symbol for hip-hop, 84-86
as testing ground for future of hip-hop, 148
Chicago Sun-Times, 73
Chicago Syndrome, 82-86
Chicago Transportation Authority, 142-45
Chicago Tribune, 73, 77, 104, 107-8
Children of Reality, 72
China Club, 72
Chinese-American Development Corporation, 120
Chi-Rock, 19, 93, 152-53, 155
Chuck D, 9, 145, 155, 14, 16
Cities
  suburban job flight, 143-44
  suburbs vs., 10-13
  "urban frontier" in, 102-6
  See also specific cities

Clarence 13X, 19
Cleveland, graffiti in, 42-
  46
"Clever", 8
CL Smooth, 16
Coker, Cheo, 79
Coltrane, John, 66
"Commercial", 8
Common Sense, 29, 70,
  93
Community change
  rap music and, 92-93
  See also Politics
Corporations, graffiti
  and, 142-43
Crain's Chicago Business,
  73
Crazy Legs (graffiti
writer), 17, 80,
  81, 114
Criticism, black-white
  differences
  concerning, 34-35
Cross Colours, 95
Cultural space, invasion
  of, 40-41
Culture
  Afrikan, 90-91
  suburbs' impact on, 12
Cypress Hill, 16, 24

Da Ghetto
  Communicator, 79
Dariens, 13-14, 18-19, 21
Das EFX, 14, 24
Davis, Mike, 31
Day, Wendy, interview
  with, 96-101

Deep, 142
"Def", 8
De La Soul, 66-67
Del the Funky
  Homosapien, 80
Dem Dare, 93
Demon, 123
Dennis, Reginald, 78
*Destruction of Black
  Civilization, The*
  (Williams), 90
Diamond D, 16
Diamond Shell, 14
Dismasters, 17
Disposable Heroes, 95
Divine Force, 17
Doc, 135
Donahue, Phil, 87
"Dope", 8
Dre, 13
Drugs, 156
  effect on black commu-
  nities, 90
Dry-Paper, 71-77

Eazy E, 67
Economy, suburbs and
inequality, 12
Emerge, 78
Emer One, 135, 138, 140
EPMD, 16
Eric B, 97
Esquire, 78
Exakto, 140
Exploitation
  of hip-hop, 82
  music industry and, 96-
  101

rap as tool of, 87-89

Faheem, 125
"Fake", 8
"Faking the funk", 80-82
Family structure, in black
    communities, 90
Fantom (graffiti writer),
113
Farell, James T., 30
Farrakhan, Abnar, 36, 37
Farrakhan, Louis, 29, 36,
    37, 38, 39,
    87, 100
"Fastest Runner on 61st
    Street, The"
    (Farrell), 30
"Fat", 7
"Five-O", 7-8
Flatliners, 16
"Fly", 8
Four Tops, The, 87
Frank, Tom, 23
Franklin, Aretha, 87
Freight trains, graffiti on,
    135-37
"Fresh", 8
"From the streets", 7
"Fuck New York", 7
Funk, faking, 80-82
Funkdoobiest, 18
Futura, 135, 136

Gangsta rap, 148
    commercialism, 13, 14
    future of, 16
    See also Rap music
Gang Starr, 16, 23, 87

"Gat", 8
Geeklove, 152
George, Nelson, 66, 78,
    82
Geto Boys, 25
Ghetto Art, 69, 70
Ghettos
    spread into suburbs, 12-
        13
    whites' visits to, 37
    See also Cities
Ghostface Killer, 16
Giant, 124
Gillespie, Dizzy, 66
G.L.O.B.E., 94
Graffiti
    all-city meetings, 114-
        16
    art and, 14
    artistic limitlessness of,
        149-50
    Chicago Wall of Fame,
        107-9
    in Cleveland, 42-46
    corporations and, 142-
        43
    on freight trains, 135-37
    health effects of spray
        paint, 46-48
    Internet message board,
        140
    interview with Warp,
        109-13
    in New York, 114
    in Philadelphia, 114-15
    police raid, 111-12
    rap analogy, 54-55
    regional variations, 138-

40
rules of, 55-59
in San Francisco, 115
in skateboard communi-
ty, 137
stylistic, 149-51
as subculture, 94-95
suburban response, 137-
38
suburb bombing, 144-
45
tags, 149
third wave, 137-38
and use of space, 48-49
use of word, 8
vandalism and, 56
in various cities, 134-35
white writers, 140-41
writers' social power,
144-45
Graffiti Groove Crew,
110
Graffiti Inc., 138
Grandmaster Flash, 99,
124
Grand Puba, 16
Grateful Dead, 147
GSXL, 69, 70

Hammer, 13
hampton, dream, 79
Hampton, Fred, 89
Harper's, 79
Hawkins, Yusef, 89
Headbanger, 16 ,
Health
  spray paint affecting,
  46-48, 127

Heavy D, 97
Heimbaugh, John, 120
Hemmingway, Ernest, 78
Hip-hop
  Chicago as symbol for,
  84-86
  Chicago as testing
  ground for future of,
  148
  Chicago journalism, 70
  commitment to, 146
  creative side of, 81-82
  Dry-Paper and, 71-77
  exploitation of, 82
  failure of journalism,
  68-69
  as high school way of
  life, 49054
  insertion of politics into,
  95
  journalism, 66-67
  in larger social context,
  152
  mental illness, 121-23
  moral center, 157-59
  morals and, 82
  movement based in, 19-
  20
  as multicultural, 153-54
  New York scene, 65-66
  parties, 125
  paying dues, 75-76
  political organizing
  around, 146-47
  publications, 69-70
  rap separated from,
  152-53
  renegades of, 93-96

tinkering, 124
whites in culture, 153-54
use of phrase, 8-9
See also Graffiti; Rap music
"Hip-hop corporation", 9
"Hip-hop nation", 9
"Hip-hopper",, use of phrase, 8-9
Hitchhiking
  paranoia, 127-28
  road survival, 128-29
Hodges, Craig, 91
Hoffer, Eric, 156
Homelessness, 117-19
Homosexuality, 133
"Hood", 7
Hopping Freight Trains in America (Littlejohn), 142
Hunter, 127-28

Ice Cube, 99
Ice-T, 13, 19
Identity, crisis of rap music, 9-10
IGT, 69, 70
Ill-State, 93
Inequality, suburbs and, 12
Institute for Positive Education, 154
Internet, graffiti message board on, 140
It's Yours, 69-70

Jackson, Jesse, 29
Jackson, Mississippi, 129-31
Jackson, Scoop, 73, 79
Jobs, cities vs. suburbs, 143-44
Johnson Publishing family, 29
Jolley, Reginald, interview with, 13-21
Journalism
  Chicago hip-hop, 70
  Dry-Paper, 71-77
  failure of hip-hop, 68-69
  hip-hop, 66-67
  publications, 69-70
JP Chill, 16
Jungle Brothers, 18
Just Ice, 16
JVC Force, 17

Kelly, R., 29
Kemelions, 98
Kenwood Academy, 31
Khamit-Kush, Indus, 90-91
Kinetic Order, 72
King, Martin Luther, 89, 145
Kool G. Rap, 14, 16
Kool Moe Dee, 158
Kozak, Eric, 55
KRS-ONE, 9, 16, 65, 67, 81, 89, 99, 151-52, 155
Kunjufu, 154
Kyle, Alex, 141

Language, abused phrases, 7-9
Large Professor, 14, 81
Latinos, graffiti writing by, 140
Lee, Parker, 125
Lee, Spike, 28
Lester, Sheena, 74, 78, 100
Liberals, 32
Littlejohn, Duffy, 142
LL Cool J, 14, 24, 158
Lord of the Flies (Golding), 108
Lords of the Underground, 94
Luke, 67
Lunch Box Law, 148
Lynn, Rashied, 29
Lyrics, in rap music, 13

"Mad", 7
Magic Mike, 99
Magic Records, 99
Maglia, Lou, 98
Mailer, Norman, 32
Malcolm X, 19, 28, 89, 96
Malone, Bonz, 78
Mannis, Deborah, 100
Mantronix, 17
Marriot, Bob, 78
Mason, Karen, 100
Masters of Ceremony, 17
Mayfield, Curtis, 87
Mayo, Kierna, 65
Mays, David, 77, 97

MC Breeze, 151
MC Eiht, 13
MC Lyte, 14, 67
Melle Mel, 87
Mental illness, in hip-hop culture, 121-23
Missionary mentality, 32, 34
Money, 131-32
Morals
  hip-hop and, 82
  hip-hop's moral center, 157-59
Morrison, Toni, 66
Mother Jones, 78
Ms., 78
MTV, 14
Multiculturalism, hip-hop and, 153-54

Nassir, 121-23
Nation, The, 79
National Review, 78
Nation of Islam, 20-21, 156-57
New Jack Enterprises, 72-73
New Republic, 79
New World Order, 92-93
New York
  Central Park, 141-42
  crews running spots, 124
  graffiti writing in, 114
  hip-hop scene, 65-66
New Yorker, The, 79

Old Dirty Bastard, 16

"Old-school", 7
O'Neal, Ronald, 72
On the Go, 69, 70
Onyx, 14, 18
Organizing, hip-hop
  political, 146-47
"Original", 8
Orko (graffiti writer), 35-
  36, 110-13, 115, 147

Padell, Bert, 97
Paris (rapper), 92
Passman, Donald, 99
Paying dues, 75-76
PE, 87, 89, 98
Pete Rock, 16
"Phat", 7
Philadelphia, graffiti writ-
  ing in, 114-15
"Phony", 8
"Play that Beat Mr. DJ",
  94
Police, as occupying
force, 89-90
Politics
  absence in rap of, 9-10
  hip-hop organizing,
    146-47
  insertion into hip-hop,
    95
  mass movements vs.
    practical organization,
    156
  political rap songs, 89
  and social division, 158
Poulson-Bryant, Scott, 78
Poverty, suburbs and, 12
Power (publisher), 135

Powers, Steve, 55n
"Practice wall", 8
PRT, 14
P-Shay, 131
Public Enemy, 24, 24, 95
Public space, suburbs'
impact on, 12-13
Punk Rock Techno, 17

Q-Tip, 59, 63
Queen Latifah, 95, 100

Race
  hip-hop and, 19-20
  See also Blacks; Racism;
Whites
Racism
  basic white perception
underlying,
    30-31
  blacks' social condition,
89-90
  encountering, 61-62
  neighborhood geogra-
phy and, 29-30
Rakim, 13, 97
Rammelzee, 147
Ranks (writer), 123-24
Rap Bandit, 79
Rap Coalition, The, 96-
101
Rap music
  Afrikan values in, 89
  as black man's man-
hood, 65
  and community change,
    92-93
  graffiti analogy, 54-55

greatest impact of, 25
hip-hop separated from,
    152-53
identity crisis, 9-10
literary gap and, 68
lyrics, 13
political songs, 89
rappers exploited, 96-
    101
record companies, 98
record sales, 22
as tool of exploitation,
    87-89
whites' miscomprehen-
    sion of, 21-27
See also Gangsta rap
Rappages, 73, 78
Rappers, exploitation of,
    96-101
Rasta 68, 135
Reading, importance of,
    78
"Real", 8
Real estate development,
in Chicago, 119-20
Rebel XD, 123
Record companies,
    nature of, 98
Red Man, 16
Reggae, 87
"Renegades of Funk,
    The", 93
"Revolutionary", 8
Riot, 152-53
Ro, Ronin, 79
Robinson, Sylvia, 99
Rogers, J.A., 90
Rolling Stone, 78

Royko, Mike, 31
RUN-DMC, 14, 97

Sabourin, Jim, 136
St. Louis, description,
    127
Salahdin, 82-85
Salsman, Dr., 61
San Francisco, graffiti
writing in, 115
Scandal (graffiti writer),
    136, 137
Schooly D, 16
Scott La Rock, 18
Scrawl Master Scarce, 49
Scribe, 95
Segregation, suburbs and,
    12
Shabazz, Betty, 29
Shakur, Tupac, 13
Shan, 24
Shecter, Jon, 77
Simmons, Russell, 97
Sir-Mix-A-Lot, 67, 97
Skateboard community,
    graffiti in, 137
"Skills", 8
Skinny Boys, 85
Slavery, 90
Slick Rick, 16
Smith, Danyel, 78-79
Smooth J. Smoothe, 99
Snoop Doggy Dog, 13,
    21
Social change, rap music
    and, 92-93
Source, The, 14, 17, 17,
    21, 27, 66, 69, 70, 72,

73, 75, 77, 78, 97,125
Space, graffiti and use of,
   48-49
Special Ed, 14, 16
Spice 1, 13, 16
Spin, 78
Spray Can Art, 107
Spray paint, health effects
   of, 46-48, 127
Stephney, Bill, 100
Step Sun Records, 100
Stony Island, 77
Stop the Violence cam-
   paign, 100
Strange, Adario, 79
Suburbs
   bombing, 144-45
   and city job losses, 143-
      44
   city vs., 10-13
   response to graffiti in,
      137-38
Subway and Elevated, 69,
   77, 79-80, 86
Super LP Raven, inter-
   view with, 147-55
Surface, Mark, 79

Tate, Greg, 78
Temptations, The, 87
Ten Tray, 86
Thomas, Lesley, interview
   with, 59-67
Thorns, Tarek, 40
Tinkering, 124
Treach, 16
Tribe, 98
Tribe Called Quest, 16

Troop, 17
TRQ, 95
"True", 8
True Believer, The
   (Hoffer), 156
True Skool, 81
"True to the game", 8
Tung Twista, 16, 54, 123,
   125
Turk, 138
Twain, Mark, 77
Twoer, Mare, 134, 138
2-Quick, 136
2000 Seasons (Armah),
   90

Ultramag, 17
"Underground", 8
Unity, 18
University of Chicago
Laboratory School,
   29
"Urban frontier", 102-6
Utne Reader, 78

Vandalism, graffiti and,
   56
Vanilla Ice, 23
Vez, 137
Vibe, 66, 78
Videos, effect on rap
music, 13
Village Voice, 66, 78

Warp (graffiti writer),
interview with,
   109-13
Warriors, 110

Washington, Harold, 29
Watts, Geoffrey, 77, 92
WBEZ, 73
WBLS, 97
What They Never Taught You in History Class (Khamit-Kush), 90-91
Whites
  anti-racist organizing, 90
  blacks' acceptance of, 39-40
  fascination with blacks, 31-33
  graffiti writing by, 140-41
  in hip-hop culture, 153-54
  rap miscomprehended by, 21-27
  response to criticism, 34-35
  visits to ghettos, 37
Whiz Kid, 94
WHPK, 14, 18, 116
"Why Is That?", 89
Why Not (rapper), 125
Wiggers, 27-31
  fascination with blacks, 31-33
Wilder, Chris, 77
Williams, Chancellor, 90
Williams, Sabrina, 22, 25
Wilson, Shane, 117-19
Wilson, William Julius, 29
Witch 1, 84
Woodson, Carter G., 90

Wright, Richard, 29

X-Clan, 24, 89, 97

"Ya know what I'm sayin?", use of phrase, 8
Young MC, 13

Zore, 136, 149
Zulu Nation, 19, 21, 93, 101